ACTIVE VANCOUVER

A Year-round Guide to Outdoor Recreation

in the City's Natural Environments

Roy Jantzen

RMB

Rocky Mountain Books
www.rmbooks.com

Library and Archives Canada Cataloguing in Publication

Jantzen, Roy, author
    Active Vancouver / Roy Jantzen.
Includes bibliographical references and index.
Issued in print and electronic formats.
ISBN 978-1-77160-079-8 (pbk.).—ISBN 978-1-77160-080-4 (epub).—
ISBN 978-1-77160-081-1 (pdf)

    1. Vancouver (B.C.)—Guidebooks. 2. Outdoor recreation—British Columbia—
Vancouver—Guidebooks. I. Title.

FC3847.18.J36 2015   917.11'33045   C2015-901008-X
                                                   C2015-901009-8

Printed in Canada

Rocky Mountain Books acknowledges the financial support for its publishing program from the Government of Canada through the Canada Book Fund (CBF) and the Canada Council for the Arts, and from the province of British Columbia through the British Columbia Arts Council and the Book Publishing Tax Credit.

This book was produced using FSC®-certified, acid-free paper, processed chlorine free and printed with vegetable-based inks.

DISCLAIMER

The actions described in this book may be considered inherently dangerous activities. Individuals undertake these activities at their own risk. The information put forth in this guide has been collected from a variety of sources and is not guaranteed to be completely accurate or reliable. Many conditions and some information may change owing to weather and numerous other factors beyond the control of the authors and publishers. Individual climbers and/or hikers must determine the risks, use their own judgment and take full responsibility for their actions. Do not depend on any information found in this book for your own personal safety. Your safety depends on your own good judgment based on your skills, education and experience.

It is up to the users of this guidebook to acquire the necessary skills for safe experiences and to exercise caution in potentially hazardous areas. The authors and publishers of this guide accept no responsibility for your actions or the results that occur from another's actions, choices or judgments. If you have any doubt as to your safety or your ability to attempt anything described in this guidebook, do not attempt it.

Active Vancouver

So many active ways to enjoy Vancouver's seawall

To those who always adventure with me: my wife Heather; my sons Christopher, Brent, Connor and Ian; and to Vi, Orv and Jennifer, who always inspire me to keep active.

Part of the fun of kayaking is getting out exploring ...

(PHOTO COURTESY OF VALERIE BELANGER)

Contents

Acknowledgements

Thank you to my colleagues, family and friends, Rick Davies, Dick Avison, Christy Dodds, Bruce Wilson, Kim McLeod and Mark Littlefield, for accompanying me on my research for this book and providing me with advice and direction.

Thank you to Patricia Thomson for your detailed editing, your nature knowledge, your advice, your friendship and for all you do in this world to connect people to nature. You are always an inspiration to me.

Thank you to Mary Whitley, for helping me ensure my Eco-Insights were understandable to readers who may have little knowledge of southwestern British Columbia.

Thank you to Rob Alexander from North Vancouver. It is Rob's nature photos that give this book the style I was looking for to ensure it felt like a genuine nature resource, as well as a recreation activity book. Other great photos of Rob's are at flickr.com/photos/northvanrob/.

Thank you to those friends who have photography businesses that generously offered their photos for this book. These include:

- Lee Halliday, who generously took the time to take a professional photo of me for the author photo and to provide some wonderful snowshoeing images. Other photos of Lee's are at leehalliday-photo.com.

- Jenn Dickie is a fantastic outdoor photographer from Squamish. Jenn provided some excellent photos for several of the activities. Additional photos of Jenn's can be found at jenndickie.com.

- Stuart McCall is a professional photographer who rows with the Delta Deas Rowing Club. He provided the often hard-to-get photos of rowing. Stuart's work can be seen at northlightimages.com

Thank you to those other friends and family who stepped forward to provide photographs. I wanted this book to reflect my community and the diversity and creativity that come from seeing the world through the eyes of others. I want to thank Lori Geosits, Christine Gaio, Shelley Frick, Phil Dubrulle, Mark Littlefield, Trevor Bonas, Terry Berezan, Mary Horton, Vi Jantzen, Sara Mitchell, Jacqueline Slagle, Jen Reilly,

Balanced rocks (PHOTO COURTESY OF CHRISTINE GAIO)

(PHOTO COURTESY OF VALERIE BELANGER)

Rorri McBlane, Brad Sills, Valerie Belanger, Cam Anderson, Brittany Coulter, Kim McLeod, Norma Ibarra, Jill Simpson, Colin Moorhead and Tourism Chilliwack.

Thank you to Terry Berezan for using his artistic eye to help me sort through so many great photos, helping me to achieve a style, design and feel for *Active Vancouver*.

Thank you to Volker Bodegom, whom I met when I thought this book was ready to send out to publishers. Volker assured me there was much more work to do and I greatly appreciated his guidance.

And thank you to my wife, Heather Avison, for encouraging me to write, for accompanying me on so many activities and for editing my political rants, my words like "cant" and my text too scant!

Metro Vancouver Overview Map

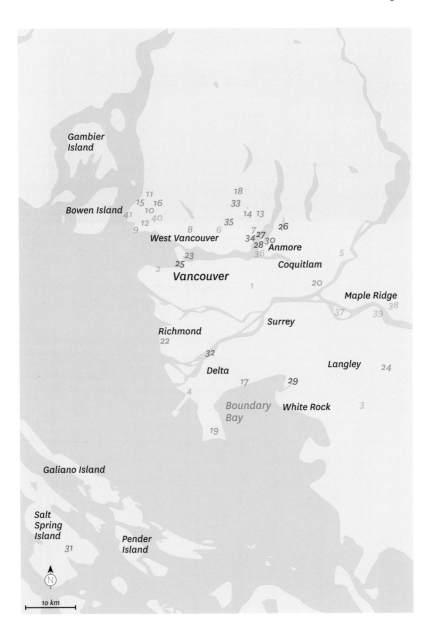

"Go Further" Overview Map

Active Vancouver:
An Introduction

"Explore," "adventure," "discover," "journey," "learn," "absorb," "grow," "be active, lively, fit and healthy": Do you identify with these words? Do they speak to something inside that feeds a desire to get outside?

These words define this book, its focus and its direction. First, let me congratulate you for picking up this book. The pages that follow will help you discover, in my opinion, many of Metro Vancouver's unique recreational gems. This city is privileged. Surrounded by green space, good planning, great infrastructure and a diverse topography of mountains, lakes, rivers, delta and ocean, the city has the components necessary for its citizens to be active. Truly experiencing Metro Vancouver's outdoors means having a variety of ways to be active, allowing you to maintain a healthy activity level throughout the seasons.

This book presents a myriad of activities, spanning multiple geographic areas and various levels of skill and effort. The chapters range from hiking and trail running to snowshoeing, cycling, paddling canoes or kayaks and picnicking at sites that require a little effort to reach. One chapter spans an array of sports, including swimming, mountain biking, rowing, paddleboarding, rock climbing and skate skiing, and leads you to a specific site for your first experience. If the thought of trying these activities for the first time is exciting, or if you are enthusiastic to learn new destinations for a familiar sport, then this book is for you. However, this book is more than a resource for learning new sports or discovering new areas – it is also about fostering an awareness of the natural environment that surrounds you.

In order to provide an educational component to help increase your environmental awareness as you undertake each adventure, this book gives an ecological insight, or Eco-Insight, associated with each activity. These provide an essential subtext to the recreational activities and aim to help you make a connection between the environment and your adventure. Different environments lend themselves to particular topics within natural history. For instance, on Bowen Island a flooded lake offers an opportunity to consider dead-standing trees and the array of wildlife "condos" they provide. One can't go to Stanley Park without some attention paid to urban-dwelling species. And a subalpine snowshoe to Dog Mountain is far more enlightening when one considers alpine survival and adaptation. Each activity outline includes a briefly elucidated theme associated with the environment that encompasses the area.

Each activity also provides a quick synopsis of distance, timing, difficulty level, elevation, transit access and surface cover. The activity pages also supply maps, as well as details about restroom facilities, specific activity-related safety considerations, equipment rentals, other points of interest to expand your day and companionship suited for the adventure. Appendices B, C, D and E all suggest activities, sorted for your potential needs. Use the final section of this book in your initial planning stage by answering questions such as:

Where do you want to go? Look through the regional sorting of activities in Appendix B.

How much effort do you want to expend? Read the tables that group activities according to level of difficulty in Appendix E.

Would you like to utilize public transit? Consider scanning the activities sorted by region tables in Appendix B.

Who would be good to join you on this activity? Suggestions for activities in appendices C and D include thoughts on appropriateness for dogs, children, teens, older adults or out-of-town visitors.

I already know much about my region, don't I? Appendix A offers an insightful, ten-question, bioregional quiz that helps gauge your knowledge and understanding about the infrastructure that surrounds and supports us.

If you engage in multiple activities, be prepared for the ubiquitous question, "What's your favourite activity?" Of course, the answer is this just isn't a fair question. To answer it you would have to compare a sunset snowshoe overlooking a world-class city with a temperate forest cycle leading to a remnant old-growth ecosystem, including lunch on a quiet river's edge. You would have to evaluate how a silent morning lake swim that takes in the scent of the surrounding forest resting

on the still water surface compares with a live music jam session at Hollyburn Lodge after a headlamp-lit snowshoe through the forest. Why would you want to compare? Well, you don't have to. Nor do you have to match a North Shore classic hike with a Fraser Valley trail run, or paddleboarding with kayaking. Instead, embrace each activity the following pages have to offer for its own sake as you expand your recreational horizons by enjoying some of the best activities available throughout Metro Vancouver.

Finally, this book offers a way to expand your experience outdoors by suggesting safety essentials for your pack, ethical considerations for the environment, volunteering opportunities associated with these areas and multimedia resources, as well as outdoor clubs and organizations open for you to join.

"As long as I live, I'll hear waterfalls and birds and winds sing. I'll interpret the rocks, learn the language of flood, storm, and the avalanche. I'll acquaint myself with the glaciers and wild gardens, and get as near the heart of the world as I can."

—John Muir, *Son of the Wilderness: The Life of John Muir*, 1945

A Recreation-in-Nature Philosophy

For a better understanding of the intent of this book, I think it would be helpful for me to explain my philosophy and experience. I have lived in Metro Vancouver for most of my life. I don't do any one sport particularly well, but I enjoy many and do them adequately enough to allow me to experience this region in multiple ways. I would call myself a generalist and I have written this book with other generalists in mind. In addition, I appreciate the diverse landscape that surrounds Metro Vancouver and know there are few large cities in the world with mountains, ocean, forests and floodplain so close to the city centre. This, combined with a diversity of preserved areas and the infrastructure to recreate in them, makes for a unique blend that, I feel, makes Metro Vancouver special.

I must add that the "specialness" that speaks to me in my outdoor recreation adventures often comes through nature. Therefore, I have designed this book to provide readers a connection to nature in whatever recreational activity they choose. My aim is to share some connections through Eco-Insights associated with each activity. Ideally, the focus of each Eco-Insight will be about connections happening in the environment that surround you while you're there. They may be historical or social, biological or conservation-based, and my hope is to inform your activity and expand your awareness. Think about how you approach the environment in which you spend your leisure time. Perhaps it offers up a challenge, provides a place to release stress, a location to think, a setting to connect with another or a way to grow. Reflecting on how you approach an environment and what the location has to offer can lead to a deeper understanding of yourself and the environment. It is my hope that providing short commentaries on species, their habitats, ecosystems and the connections between them will help enrich your experience and expand your curiosity.

Ultimately, observation and awareness really are the subtext to this book. While carrying out an activity, take time to observe your

BC's provincial bird, the Stellar's jay (PHOTO COURTESY OF TERRY BEREZAN)

surroundings. Train yourself to see more than the general, to focus on the details, to listen – really listen – and to read signs. You will almost certainly pass scattered feathers, a tree base where a squirrel fed recently, a nibbled branch, tracks in the sand or tunnels in the snow. Commit to learning ten common birdcalls. Do this with an app on your phone, downloadable audio files online and/or a bird guide to the most common birds in your area. I guarantee it will enrich your run, cycle, hike or snowshoe if you connect that sound above your head to a golden crowned kinglet calling for a mate in the trees above or a Pacific wren letting you know you are moving through his territory.

So whatever your motivation – getting your heart rate up, building muscle, burning calories, breathing fresh air, socializing or exploring – this book is designed to lead you to some of Metro Vancouver's very special places and to facilitate your understanding of the wider significance these places hold.

How to Use This Book

Each activity has icons to allow for a quick assessment. The icon designs allow you to quickly match the activity to your motivations for the day. Before choosing where to go and what you want to do there, it is valuable to think about the time available; the energy level or capabilities of your party; the weather; the composition of the group (e.g., beginners, children, older adults); the distance you want to travel to get to the activity; whether your focus is on exercise, socializing or immersion in nature, or a combination thereof; and the equipment required.

Activity Headings

The following are the activity headings used in the book:

Activity Highlight: The introduction for each activity is the activity highlight. This provides the key features and focus of the activity. I have framed these in relation to the region, to people and the purpose of the activity.

Directions: With GPS, Google Maps, smartphones and other devices, I have made the assumption that getting to the activity location will be relatively easy. Unless directions to the site are complex, I have primarily outlined directions *specific to the site* where the activity takes place.

Notes: This section is for important, useful or extraneous information that may add to the experience, including the following.

- *Transit & Transportation:* This heading is used only for those activities where additional information is required for transit or transportation. Buses that come every two hours and/or operate only in the summer, or transport that includes a ferry are examples of the type of information incorporated under this heading.

- *Maps:* The maps for each activity should help you visualize the route and put it in perspective in relation to the wider geographic area. Most, but not all, activities have a map.

- *Restrooms:* For all sites, I try to provide the most up-to-date information on where restrooms are located, but note that depending on the season, they are not always open. In addition, I'd suggest adding toilet paper to your pack, as park restrooms might not be fully stocked.

- *Safety:* There is a Safety & Security Planning section in this chapter, outlining general safety, while several activities themselves provide extra information where safety is required. Be sure to read both prior to planning your activities.

- *Timing:* For some activities, I discuss the best time of year to engage in it, others the best time of the week, or even the best time of day.

- *Company:* I think some activities lend themselves well to challenging a teenager, turning on the wonder in a child, offering a visitor a chance to experience a classic part of British Columbia or a place to make an impression on a date.

- *Dogs:* It's great to take your dog with you while recreating, but it isn't always appropriate. Most activities in this book provide you with options. For any activity, always keep your dog under control and pick up after them. Many sites covered in this book are critical wildlife habitats and our coastal marshes attract millions of migratory birds. Dogs can affect birds that are nesting or foraging and they can alter the behaviour of species. Be aware that wild animals and birds use additional energy avoiding conflict with your pet and that energy needs replenishing. If the species happens to be a bird that is getting set to migrate to South America shortly, for example, then that energy expenditure is incredibly important. Note that Appendix C has a list of sites that are best suited for dogs.

- *Of Interest:* Many places in this book have interesting features associated with them. I used this heading to help ensure the reader knows about them with the intention of adding to the experience.

- *Rentals/Tips:* I have made suggestions on rentals or tips available where appropriate. However, businesses do change and what is available to rent in one season may not be available the next. Be sure to plan accordingly by contacting the suggested businesses first and asking if a reservation for rental equipment is required. Mountain Equipment Co-op offers rentals for most equipment.

Eco-Insight: I love recreating in all the areas outlined in this book. It is the Eco-Insight section, though, that inspired me to write it. This section offers brief, 250 – 300 word articles on the connections between the ecosystems you are recreating in and the species that inhabit them. I hope they inspire you to learn more, and if they do, please don't hesitate to contact me and let me know how.

Other Area Interests: These ideas help you expand your day with other, complementary activities or experiences in the general area.

Map Graphic: The maps in the book are for guidance and help provide a visual overview of the activity. Suggestions for more detailed activity maps are often in the notes.

Overnight snow before a clear day always makes a magical scene.
(PHOTO COURTESY OF JENN DICKIE)

Activity Planning

When it comes to planning an outdoor activity, there are a few things you should keep in mind.

Outdoor Ethics

The philosophy of this book is to tread lightly, respect the environment you are recreating in and, when possible, make it better because you're there. The activities in this book take you to some sites where wildlife may be abundant. I cannot stress enough how important it is to adhere to the following rules:

Pack out What You Pack in: Take all litter with you (and consider removing some that isn't yours) or place it in bins that may be on site.

Don't Feed Animals: Do not feed animals human food. This includes the whisky jacks, ravens and chipmunks habituated to people at the

Keep the animals' best interests in mind when considering feeding them. (PHOTO COURTESY OF ROB ALEXANDER)

summits of most local mountaintops. If you disagree with the no feeding rule, then please pack birdseed or *unsalted* nuts, if you must. Our snack and lunch items of potato chips, granola bars, bread, processed baloney or cheese may interest animals now but can have a profoundly negative impact on their survival later in the winter.

Respect the Wild: Avoid disturbing nesting birds and wildlife. A basic rule is that if you can tell you are affecting an animal's behaviour, back off – you are too close. Use binoculars, the zoom lens on your camera or pull out your glasses instead of moving closer.

Leave Plants for Wildlife: Try a few berries (taste is one of the senses we seldom get to use outside and it really can add to your experience), but remember that wildlife utilize plants and berries as food too. Don't take too much and avoid damaging or removing plants.

Stay on the Trails: Cross-cutting leads to erosion and degrades the landscape. Respect trail closures.

Gotta Go? Be Discreet: I have tried to outline where restrooms (this includes outhouses) are for the activities. However, if you are out and can't wait and you "gotta go," then consider the following: do your business at least 45 metres from a stream, body of water or trailside. If toilet paper is involved, don't leave it – that's disgusting. Dig a hole, do your business and cover it up, or consider packing a plastic bag to pack out the paper.

Consider Getting Involved: Both Metro Vancouver Parks and BC Parks are always looking for people interested in protecting the land they manage. They often have environmental stewardship projects, public events and educational programs that require volunteers. Consider immersing yourself in an area through volunteering. For more information, do a web search on stewardship and volunteering opportunities for BC Parks, Metro Vancouver Parks or other nonprofit, nature-focused organizations in Vancouver.

Weather

Weather, and associated precipitation, in Metro Vancouver varies considerably depending on proximity to the North Shore Mountains. The microclimate for a trail run in North Vancouver's Lynn Headwaters

Regional Park compared to Brunswick Point in Delta is substantial. Similarly, there is three times the amount of rain on a bicycle ride in the upper Seymour Valley (approximately 3000 mm/year) than there is biking at Point Roberts (approximately 1000 mm/year), so consider the huge differences in weather associated with this region. Check the local forecast when deciding on the best activity for the weather. Depending on the activity, you may also want to check the mountain forecast or websites for the local ski hills that update weather forecasts frequently.

activevancouver.ca

The website that complements this book is activevancouver.ca. The site provides updates on activities that have changed since the publication of this book. It also suggests other complementary recreational activities and Eco-Insights, and provides additional safety tips, links that complement the subject matter and offers news on opportunities to get involved in Metro Vancouver's recreational areas. In addition, it has author updates and contact information, social media sharing and bonus materials such as videos, audio files, photos and maps that support and extend your experience.

Ultimately, the vision is to make the website a place where readers can provide current updates on trail conditions, share their activity happenings with others and offer suggestions to improve the overall experiences of fellow recreationalists.

Go Further

Decide on how far you wish to travel for your activity. At least one activity in each section of this book leads you *out of* the Metro Vancouver region and in to other areas. I am breaking my own rules in trying to keep this a Metro Vancouver book, but then I also want to encourage readers to expand their repertoire of geographical locations to include areas like the Squamish-Whistler corridor, the Gulf Islands, Sunshine Coast and Fraser Valley. Perhaps these are the beginning of a second, wider-reaching edition, but for now, I was just so enthusiastic about them that I couldn't pass them by!

Safety & Security Planning

Being prepared for any outdoor activity is the key to safely enjoying the outdoors. Use the following list as a guide to ensure preparedness for your activity. You can photocopy or cut out the following pages to put in your pack permanently.

- Check the trail or park conditions prior to your recreational activity by calling the responsible organization for the area or looking on their website for updates.

- Tell someone about the trails you intend to be on and your expected time of return (all mileage and time outlined in this book is *return time*). Consider putting a note on the dash of your car if you haven't told anyone of your absence.

- Be prepared for all weather conditions and know the current forecast.

- Stay on signed trails, obtain a map and check it frequently while on the trails.

- Darkness comes quickly in valleys and forested areas; allow time to return before dark.

- Turn back if the weather worsens or the activity becomes too strenuous.

- If lost, stay put and wait for help.

- Know what to do if you surprise a bear (no direct eye contact, no running). Look down and to the side, back away slowly and be loud. On the other hand, if it is a cougar, be large, loud and intimidating.

- Although not common in the areas discussed in this book, watch for ticks around your ankles, waist and hair.

- Carry the ten activity safety essentials listed below in your backpack, pannier or boat dry bag.

Ten Essentials for Activity Safety

The gear you bring will depend, for the most part, on the activity you choose and the amount of time you expect to be out. Factors such as the weather, terrain, who is accompanying you, how far you are from assistance or whether you want the flexibility to extend your activity will all influence your decision. Whether you are using a daypack, a pannier or a hydration or hip pack, consider the following when preparing for your outing or, rather, should I say your insurance policy for your outing!

Keep the following at the bottom of your pack and leave it there, but check it before you depart for the day:

❑ Flashlight/headlamp – with reliable and/or extra batteries.

❑ Extra food and water – at a minimum, a 500-ml water bottle, Gatorade crystals and a few high-energy food bars.

❑ Extra warm and waterproof clothing (think layers) – buy a small stuff sack and, at a minimum, put in a wool toque, fleece sweater, gloves, wool socks, light rain jacket and pants (no jeans or cotton).

❑ First aid kit and sun protection – know what's in it and how to use it. Consider a small ready-made kit with a booklet, as well as a minimum of SPF 15 sunscreen and hat.

❑ Pocket knife or multipurpose tool – not just for opening the wine and cutting the brie. It has infinite uses!

❑ Fire – fire-starter candle with waterproof matches or a lighter.

❑ Signal device – connect a whistle to all the packs you use.

❑ Emergency shelter – a large, orange, "multipurpose" garbage bag (cheap), thermal bag (also cheap) or a corded siltarp (pricey but small and light) would serve as a shelter.

The final two items you should add to your pack on the day you head out:

❑ Map and communication – get a map and compass or a GPS (and extra batteries) and train yourself on how to use them; bring a fully charged cellphone. For the North Shore there is a great map titled North Shore Trail Map – GPS-based – 1:20,000 waterproof.

Available at Mountain Equipment Co-op, it covers many of the activities in this book.

❑ Personal items – bring glasses (sun, vision), any required medication, identification and an extra set of car keys (ideally connected to another activity partner). Know your plan and tell someone else about it (who you're with, where you're going and when you expect to return).

In addition, here is one more thing to consider: bring a child or teenager if you can! A partner not only adds another level of safety but bequeathing an attitude of a healthy lifestyle and connection to natural areas will help young people develop a lifelong interest in the outdoors – this can only be a good thing!

Safety Equipment Specific for Water Activities

When paddling in a kayak or canoe, be sure to carry the proper safety gear. This checklist will help in your planning:

❑ personal flotation devices (PFDs) fitted properly for each person;

❑ sound-signalling device;

❑ tow/throw line;

❑ bailer or pump;

❑ paddle float;

❑ headlamps;

❑ spare paddle or oar;

❑ knife;

❑ first aid kit;

❑ thermos with hot tea;

❑ change of clothes or wetsuit/drysuit;

❑ mobile phone in a waterproof case.

Quick Safety Check for Proceeding

When you are engaged in an activity and trying to decide whether to proceed further, a simple checklist can remind you of the key factors to consider: those you are with, the weather and the terrain in relation to the conditions. You can evaluate each with a good, mediocre or poor.

Considerations	Good	Mediocre	Poor
Weather	Green	Yellow	Red
Participants	Green	Yellow	Red
Terrain	Green	Yellow	Red

One Yellow = Proceed with Caution
Two Yellows = Stop, Reflect and Re-evaluate
One Red = Stop, Reflect and Re-evaluate

Suggested Reading, Resources, Media & Organizations

The following books are for the general reader and, although they can go into much detail, the authors always connect the detail to the greater environment that surrounds us. I hope I have been able to do the same within this book.

Books

Natural History

Cannings, R.J., and S.G. Cannings. *British Columbia: A Natural History*. Vancouver: Greystone Books, 1996.

———. *The BC Roadside Naturalist*. Vancouver: Greystone Books, 2002.

Murray, A., and D.P. Blevins. *A Nature Guide to Boundary Bay*. Delta, BC: Nature Guides BC, 2006.

Parkinson, A. *Nature Vancouver. Parks and Nature Places around Vancouver*. Madeira Park, BC: Harbour Publishing, 2009.

Ocean & Ecology

Butler, R.W. *The Jade Coast: Ecology of the North Pacific Ocean*. Toronto: Key Porter Books, 2003.

Glavin, T. *The Last Great Sea. A Voyage through the Human and Natural History of the North Pacific Ocean*. Vancouver: Greystone, 2003.

Harbo, R. *Whelks to Whales: Coastal Marine Life of the Pacific Northwest*. Vancouver: Harbour, 1999.

Plants & Trees

Pojar, J., and A. MacKinnon. *Plants of Coastal British Columbia*. Vancouver: Lone Pine, 1994.

Suzuki, D.T., R. Bateman, W. Grady, and the David Suzuki Foundation. *Tree: A Life Story*. Vancouver: Greystone Books, 2004.

Birds & Mammals

Baron, N., and J. Acorn. *Birds of Coastal British Columbia: And the Pacific Northwest Coast*. Edmonton: Lone Pine, 1997.

Butler, R. *The Great Blue Heron: A Natural History and Ecology of a Seashore Sentinel*. Vancouver: UBC Press, 1997.

Dunn, J.L., and J. Alderfer. *National Geographic Field Guide to the Birds of North America, Sixth Edition*. Washington, DC: National Geographic Society, 2011.

Eder, T., and D. Pattie. *Mammals of British Columbia*. Edmonton: Lone Pine, 2001.

Sibley, D.A. *The Sibley Guide to Bird Life and Behavior*. New York: Knopf, 2009.

Geology

Clague, J.J., and B. Turner. *Vancouver, City on the Edge: Living with a Dynamic Geological Landscape*. Vancouver: Tricouni Press, 2003.

Multimedia Resources

iBird Pro: This app for Android, iOS and Kindle offers bird sounds, detailed information and identification photos.

Washington Wildflowers: This app for iOS and Android mobile devices covers 870 common wildflowers, shrubs and vines found in Washington and British Columbia. The majority of species included are native, but introduced species common to the region are also covered.

Star Walk: With this iOS app, night sky constellations come "alive" at your fingertips just by lifting your iPad or smartphone to the sky.

Bird Songs of Canada's West Coast: John Neville's CD, available on iTunes, provides examples of bird calls and sounds.

Peterson Birds – A Field Guide to Birds of North America: A guide to

North America's bird sounds provides a very wide array of different species. Available on CD or on iTunes.

Quirks and Quarks on CBC and *Radiolab* on NPR: Both these radio programs/podcasts offer information that complements activities in nature. Both are entertaining and written for a broad spectrum of listeners.

Suggested Organizations for Geographic or Natural History in British Columbia

If the Eco-Insights in this book inspire you to learn more, the following Metro Vancouver organizations can lead you further:

- Stanley Park Ecology Society;
- Lynn Canyon Ecology Centre;
- Pacific Museum of the Earth;
- Richmond Nature House;
- Beaty Biodiversity Museum;
- Vancouver Aquarium's wet lab programs;
- George C. Reifel Migratory Bird Sanctuary;
- Orphaned Wildlife Rehabilitation Society (OWL);
- BC Nature Federation;
- Vancouver Natural History Society (sections include Marine Biology, Birding, Botany, Geology, Conservation and Photography);
- Young Naturalists Clubs;
- Geological Survey of Canada (the store in downtown Vancouver with topographic maps).

Suggested Outdoor Activity Clubs & Organizations

Mec.ca has a community website that provides detailed information on outdoor activity clubs around British Columbia. A selection for Metro Vancouver includes:

- Vancouver Regional Outdoor Club;

- Inside Edge Club;
- Varsity Outdoor Club;
- Vancouver Outdoor Club;
- Alpine Club of Canada – Vancouver Section;
- Burnaby Canoe & Kayak Club;
- Federation of Mountain Clubs of BC;
- North Shore Hikers;
- North Vancouver Outdoors Club;
- Sea Kayak Association of British Columbia.

Trail Running

"Adopt the pace of nature, her secret is patience."

—Ralph Waldo Emerson, American Poet, 1803 – 1882

Metro Vancouver has such a diversity of trails, it's no wonder runners are moving from pavement to dirt with such frequency. In fact, the hammering force of running itself may also be leading people to softer ground. Trail running provides a different type of workout than, say, the classic Vancouver Seawall run. This is not just because of the coffee shops you don't pass but because your body has to be more "on." Cruise control doesn't work when trail running. Subtler muscles are involved to fine-tune balance, the brain works double-time to assess where best to step and at what speed and the body shifts on its axis to maneuver over awkward obstacles. Running among trees feels faster, just as cars appear speedier on narrow roads versus wide ones.

This chapter outlines seven exceptional trail runs in a selection of unique environments. They vary in length (5 – 15 km), in difficulty level and in running surface. When running at Locarno Beach's low tide, for instance, it would probably be wise to use older running shoes due to the saltwater puddles you'll be hopping over. Brunswick Point, on the other hand, has firm gravel and is potentially in full sun, so plan accordingly. Conversely, the most sun you can expect at Lynn Loop is sun-filtered rays through fir, cedar and hemlock trees. Burnaby Lake leads you past so many different user groups sharing the park you will find many reasons to stop and watch, while Minnekhada Regional Park's user groups are mostly of the avian kind. Certain runs are especially good in certain seasons. In the spring, running at Crippen Regional Park on Bowen Island probably means you can watch nesting birds in wildlife trees near the lake, whereas in the fall, Campbell Valley Regional Park provides a diversity of deciduous trees changing colours for you to run below. Diversity is a splendid thing.

Trail running involves some uncertainty, which you should be prepared for. Expect uneven terrain, sudden rises and drops, unseen roots easily clipped with your shoe and rocks that cause your foot to plant askew – and as we all know, injuries hurt! Your pace should be slower than when you are on pavement, so the run will feel longer than the equivalent distance on a road. See trail running as more about the process of the run, not the time and distance covered. For complete enjoyment of your trail run, please take extra caution. Here are a few points to consider when moving at speed along the trails:

- *Run with a Friend:* Consider trail running as a separate sport to urban running. The risks of injury in an area you consider serene may also mean few people coming by if you happen to twist an ankle and require help.

- *Be Multisensory:* Wearing headphones eliminates a key sensory input when running. It doesn't allow for your full attention on the trail. Surprising wildlife, not seeing critical impediments and surrounding yourself in man-made sounds will increase your chances of injury.

- *Eyes on the Trail:* Use a natural break to take in the beauty of the trail. Don't hesitate to walk or stop. If you don't slow down, turning your head to take in a scenic view may mean missing a critical step. Watch in front of you and don't overthink where you are about to step. The brain, and your subconscious, will connect the multisensory information coming in for the planting of your foot – it's amazing really! This mind-body connection is critical to successful trail running and will improve with time if you start out easy and then move to progressively more difficult runs. An example from the runs in this chapter would see you progressively increase from the flat, wide and soft Burnaby Lake run to the more difficult Minnekhada run (not as flat and with more roots, twists and turns), then on to a more difficult run such as Lynn Loop. Depending on your ability, the amount of time or number of runs at each stage will vary.

- *Equipment:* Bring a cellphone and water (think of these as being safe and safer), but don't carry them in your hands. Think hydration packs, hip packs, water belts or pockets over carrying items in your hands. Trail running shoes, in my opinion, are not strictly necessary, but they are sturdier and can give added traction.

Tree-lined trails along Burnaby Lake

If trail running becomes a complement to your wider recreational activities, then you might want to take the sport to another level. Southwestern British Columbia provides countless opportunities for trail running races if competing motivates you. Groups and clubs specific to this sport offer another option for involvement. If you are fortunate to have trails that link your home and work, then it may become a form of commuting to work (access to showers at the worksite being an important factor!). For me, running trails has also given me a different way to explore natural areas when I travel. The sport leads me to connect my desire to experience the natural world with my need for exercise.

Burnaby Lake Regional Park Trail Loop

Distance: 11 km
Time: 1 – 1.5 hrs.
Level: easy
Grade: minimal < 5 m
Public Transit Routes: 110, 134, 144
Surface: gravel/bark mulch

Activity Highlight

Can you reconnect with nature without leaving an urban city? You can here in the centre of Burnaby. This banana-shaped park provides plenty of space to get lost (not literally, but figuratively) in nature. Knowing it's sandwiched between highways 1 and 7 makes it even more amazing that this area is a vital haven for wildlife. You will find solace among

While at Burnaby Lake, take time to climb the tower and walk the dock near the nature house. This is a busy wildlife area at any time of year.

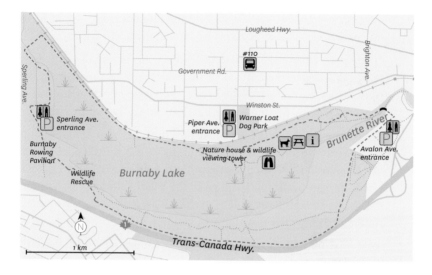

the blackberry or salmonberry thickets, amid the Labrador tea and the Indian plum. So feast upon the wildlife (again, not literally) that surrounds you and take a guess, by reading the Eco-Insight below, at what else you could do here besides a trail run.

Directions

When planning your run, choose your direction around Burnaby Lake and your entrance to the park (see Notes below). There are multiple entrances to this park. These include off Winston Street, at Piper Avenue on the north side; off Glencarin Drive on the southwest side; at Avalon Avenue on the east side; and at the Burnaby Sports Complex on the west side off Sperling Avenue.

Notes

Maps: These are available online or free at Metro Vancouver Parks.

Restrooms: These are located at multiple points around the park and at each of the entrances described above.

Timing: Burnaby Lake has many facilities that are available all year so this activity is appropriate in any season.

Dogs: Pets should be on a leash while on all park trails. An off-leash dog park is available at Warner Loat Park at the north entrance.

Of Interest: Due to the myriad of wildlife, this is one of your easier places in Metro Vancouver to see beavers (close to sunset from the wildlife viewing tower), coyotes (near the playing fields at sunrise or sunset) and birds nesting (in the bird boxes near the Nature House).

The Nature House also allows you to feed the birds here. Staff sell grain outside the Nature House. Their reasoning for this is to educate people who do feed birds to do it with nutritious food and not bread (in any form). Donations for the grain go to the Wildlife Rescue Association located on the southwest end of the lake. This is a great place to share the joy of feeding ducks with young children.

As a final note of interest, the boggy environment makes the trail around the lake soft and easy on your joints.

Eco-Insight: Dredging at Burnaby Lake

Burnaby Lake Regional Park is a celebrated example of a park whose stakeholders seek to find a balance between community recreation and nature. Don't leave this park without noticing its leisure and

LEFT: *Burnaby Lake is one of Metro Vancouver's easiest places to see Wood Ducks.*
RIGHT: *Don't be surprised to see western painted turtles sunning themselves at lakeside.* (PHOTOS COURTESY OF ROB ALEXANDER)

environmental features – the Nature House; a wildlife viewing tower; a wharf where children feed birdseed to ducks and canoeists launch their boats; wood duck nest boxes; soccer fields; an ice rink and an equestrian centre, not to mention the Burnaby Wildlife Rescue Association and the Burnaby Rowing Club. This is truly a model for a multiple-use park!

It's worth discussing a recent debate over how best to find this balance between urban use and natural space. In the spring of 2011, Burnaby Lake was successfully dredged and the city removed 180,000 cubic metres of sediment. Without dredging, the lake would have slowly become a marsh, so park users, such as the Burnaby Rowing Club, were vocal about the lake remaining (it being difficult to row sculls in a marsh). However, the provincial Ministry of the Environment raised concerns about the safety of one inhabitant that lived in the lake – the red-listed western painted turtle. In British Columbia, when a species is red-listed, it means it is endangered or threatened and may be facing imminent extirpation (loss from the area) or extinction, if limiting factors are not reversed. That meant the dredging could not go forward unless a way was found to protect the red-listed turtles. The balance? Dredging contractors waited for the turtles to hibernate, which they do by burying themselves into the sediment for the winter. Using ground-penetrating radar, workers devised a way to detect and tag the turtles on the lake bottom. Ultimately, the turtle management plan was successful. The species is still found in the park, rowers still row and the sediment that was removed became the base for sports fields on the west side of Kensington Avenue. The project was lauded for demonstrating excellence in engineering, innovation and environmental protection.

Other Area Interests

While in Burnaby, you may also wish to visit other scenic park or natural areas. These include Deer Lake (about a 5-km loop) and Burnaby Mountain for panoramic views and multiple trails. Burnaby is also home to Simon Fraser University and UniverCity – one of Metro Vancouver's most sustainably built communities.

Locarno Beach at Low Tide

Distance: 5 – 10 km
Time: 45 min. – 2 hrs.
Level: easy
Grade: minimal < 5 m
Public Transit Routes: 4, 84, C19
Surface: packed sand

Activity Highlight

Not many places allow you to run *below* the tideline for an hour or more, but on the right day, at the right time, this is one of them. Locarno is known for its volleyball, barbeques, sandy beach and seaside cycling, but if your timing is right, you can run northwest on the tidal flats for a good distance. In fact, it will appear you can run most the way out to the container ships in Burrard Inlet. This is among the more popular beaches in Vancouver, but be aware that if you run too far west you may come upon another popular one – the clothing-optional Wreck Beach.

Directions

Once you get down onto the sand flats, run in any direction your legs wish to go and toward the furthest sand you can see. Running northwest will likely provide the longest distance.

Locarno, looking toward Vancouver when the tide is in
(PHOTO COURTESY OF LORI GEOSITS)

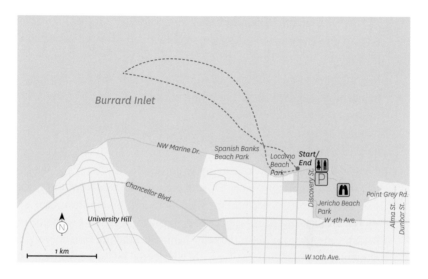

Notes

Maps: These aren't required for this run.

Restrooms: These are available next to the sea-walk food kiosk at Locarno Beach.

Safety: Know the tidal times and don't be caught out on the sand flats with ocean water coming around behind you and cutting you off from the shore.

Timing: Run only at *low tide*! The critical piece of this Active Vancouver run is to plan it on a low tide. The lowest daytime low tides are around the summer solstice (June 20 or 21) and the spring/fall equinoxes. Look also at the low tides that are associated with a full or new moon. Did you know that there is a connection between the moon cycle and tides? If you want to know more, read the Eco-Insight for Lighthouse Park Forest and Ocean Edge Loop (page 87). Canadian Tidal Prediction tables are available at tides-marees.gc.ca.

Dogs: Canine companions must be on-leash in the park area but off-leash on the sand flats. This is a great run for dogs and among the largest recreational expanses in the city!

Of Interest: Skimboarding has become a popular scene along Metro

Vancouver beaches. When the tide is out, saltwater puddles appear to scream for someone to hydroplane over them on a board – an activity perhaps for another time.

Rentals/Tips: Use an old pair of running shoes on the beach, as they will get wet and dirty as you hop (in your best gazelle-ish stride) over those saltwater puddles in the sand!

Eco-Insight: Great Blue Herons

Greater Vancouver provides many opportunities to observe a distinctive species. Seemingly spawned from prehistoric pterosaurs, our great blue heron (GBH) is a common sight here and on southwestern BC shores. Of the three subspecies of GBH in North America, two reside in British Columbia. Because they don't migrate, and are thus more vulnerable to declining habitat, both are considered by the BC Ministry of Environment to be blue-listed, or "species of special concern." It's unlikely you will see other blue-listed animals in British Columbia as easily as you can find our GBH. For perspective, consider other BC blue-listed animals such as the mountain beaver, tailed frog, marbled murrelet, snowy owl or Roosevelt elk. How often do you see these species?

With this perspective in mind, consider their place in the web of life. Colony-nesting herons are located in several Greater Vancouver locations, including Stanley Park and the Tsawwassen bluffs. It takes 100 days to lay their eggs, incubate them and raise their young with food such as intertidal fish and invertebrates, as well as rodents, frogs and snakes from farmlands. In turn, untended eggs or young chicks are food for bald eagles, hawks, ravens and crows.

(PHOTO COURTESY OF LORI GEOSITS)

Great blue heron in flight (PHOTO COURTESY OF ROB ALEXANDER)

On your run, watch for herons standing perfectly still as they feed in shallow water. What do you have in common with the GBH? You are both top predators in a food chain and as such you both are subject to higher levels of toxins in your diets. Why is that? Effluent from aquaculture operations and pesticide-containing runoff from farms and suburban neighbourhoods flow into our rivers, streams and sloughs, contaminating the plants and animals that live in those waters. Plants are known as primary producers because they use the sun's energy to grow. Primary consumers eat plants, secondary consumers eat primary consumers, tertiary consumers eat secondary consumers and so on up the food chain. At each progressive level, toxins concentrate in the consuming organism, so organisms that eat their meals higher up on the chain are subject to toxin bioaccumulation, making them more at risk of harm from the toxins.

Other Area Interests

About 3.5 km from the beach is a lunch place that is a Vancouver institution. Have lunch at the Naam (West 4th and Macdonald). It is among the most famous of Vancouver's vegetarian restaurants. If you haven't visited UBC's Museum of Anthropology, this is also highly recommended as an indoor extension to the day.

Campbell Valley Regional Park in Fall Colours

Distance: 5 – 10 km
Time: 1 – 2 hrs.
Level: easy
Grade: minimal < 68 m
Public Transit Routes: 531, C63
Surface: bark mulch/dirt/gravel

Activity Highlight

Close your eyes and focus…fall leaves are underfoot, a multitude of colours hang overhead and a slight breeze skirts around trees on a forested trail. Can you smell it? Or hear the rustling sound? Can you feel the fall leaves crunch and kick away as you run? Often we think of running as a physical act – its structure, form, pace and cadence. I suggest running is also the environment encompassing, and maybe even cradling, you. Its aroma, resonance and vibration provide you with an external sensory experience that makes each run unique. Campbell Valley is an autumn running sensory experience savoured like, well, like a fine wine.

Directions

Take 200th Street in Langley south to 20th, 16th or 4th, depending on where you wish to start. There are 15 different entrances to this park. Maps are usually available at the kiosks at the north or south valley entrances. Once there, choose the direction and the specific trails for your run, though I suggest the scenic route outlined below.

Notes

Maps: You can find maps for the trails online or free at Metro Vancouver Parks. The most scenic route is on the Little River loop, Ravine, Vine Maple and Meadow trails. A longer run incorporates the southern end of the Shaggy Mane (also used for horses) trail. Plan your run to go by

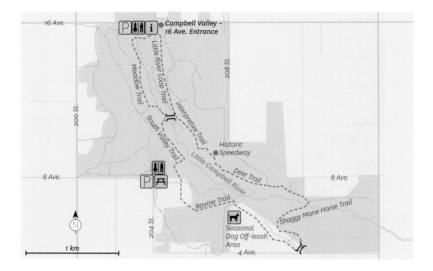

the historic Langley speedway. The track seems very out of place today (as it's surrounded by trees and trails), but it did host stock car races from 1963 to 1984, including NASCAR races.

Restrooms: These are available at the north, south and east entrances of the park.

Timing: This run is best in the fall (late September to mid-October) because of the beautiful fall colours of the bigleaf maples and other deciduous trees that surround the trails.

Company: If you choose to do this run on a sunny fall day and the leaves have turned colour, bring your favourite photographer, as the area (and you in all your galloping glory, of course) will be very photogenic.

Dogs: Your furry pal should be on-leash while on all park trails. An off-leash and dog-run area is located in the south part of the park off 4th Avenue.

Of Interest: Interpretive trails are in the park – be aware that some of the signs are interesting enough to distract you from your running technique! This park is easy on the joints due to soft trails that criss-cross it.

Forest steps (PHOTO COURTESY OF MARK LITTLEFIELD)

Eco-Insight: Fall Colours

The fall leaves at Campbell Valley Regional Park have always been a draw for me. The deciduous trees of red alder, black cottonwood and bigleaf maple all turn colour between late September and mid-October. When you catch it on a sun-drenched, dry, fall day, there is nothing like a run among the leaves. But what's really going on here? The green colours of summer are a product of the mineral magnesium residing in chlorophyll – the chemical responsible for photosynthesis. As days shorten, the trees shut down this food-making factory and begin the transition to living off their stored energy. As the green fades, other chemical colours show through in reds, oranges and yellows.

Devil's club provides great colour to West Coast forests.
(PHOTO COURTESY OF TERRY BEREZAN)

The colours have been there all along, just masked by the strong green of chlorophyll in the summer!

As the trees move into winter mode, they drop their leaves to save energy. The leaves, in turn, provide necessary nitrogen for the soil, food for decomposers and they create another annual layer for the rich organic soil (nature's compost!) to foster new life. Do you know how long this process has been going on in Campbell Valley? If you guessed about 11,000 years, the time of the last ice age retreat, then kudos to you. On your run, look for clay-cliff faces that show a line between the rich, dark-brown, organic soil and the sandy, light-coloured, mineral soil. The thickness of the dark layer is…you guessed it, about 11,000 years of leaf-falling, nutrient-enriched compost! Ahhhh, breathe in the fall leaves!

Other Area Interests

Fort Langley is usually a field trip many of us Vancouverites embarked upon as children in elementary school. If you haven't been there since then, or have never visited, it is worth some extra time while in the Langley area.

Brunswick Point & Beyond

Distance: 8 – 15 km
Time: 1 – 2.5 hrs.
Level: moderate
Grade: minimal < 5 m
Public Transit Route: 620 (see Notes)
Surface: gravel dyke

Activity Highlight

"You live all the way out in Ladner?!" That was a common comment made by friends when I lived in the neighbourhood of Brunswick Point. It seemed as if anything south of Vancouver's Marine Drive was a hinterland. Perhaps that is why you are likely to have this area to yourself, or shared only with local dog walkers. The fact is Vancouver is spoiled – picturesque and enchanting corners frame the city. Therefore, when you want an activity that expands your geographic horizons, consider the Ladner "hinterlands" of Brunswick Point. It's flat and provides a 360-degree view of the North Shore Mountains, Vancouver Island, the San Juan Islands and Mount Baker – and you will take it all in unaccompanied by the crowds.

Directions

Take the Massey Tunnel to Ladner Trunk Road and then to River Road until its end. The dyke trail heads south to Brunswick Point then east past farms on your left to a gate at the 4-km mark. Return for an 8-km run or continue past the gate, the train tracks and across the Roberts Bank coal port jetty road. The trail continues on the other side until it meets the BC Ferries causeway (another 3.5 km). Turn around here for a full 15-km run. If coming by bus, you will be doing this in the opposite direction. See the Notes below.

Notes

Transit & Transportation: The only way to take public transit to this site is by taking the #620 bus to the Tsawwassen ferry and getting off

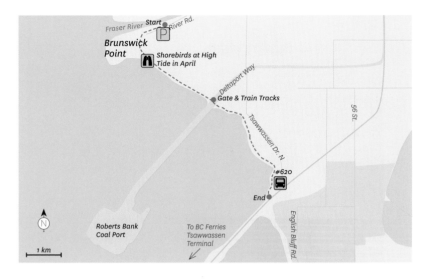

at Highway 17 and Tsawwassen Drive. It's a short walk to the dyke from this stop. Note this will mean your trail run will be in the opposite direction as written in the directions above.

Maps: These are sparse for this area. I suggest printing one from a satellite photo off Google Maps.

Restrooms: These are not available anywhere on this activity route.

Timing: All year is good, but an especially good time for this run is in the third week of April (and more specifically at high tide) as it is the peak of spring migration for shorebirds, and millions pass through this spot on their way north (see Eco-Insight below).

Company: Do you know anyone just getting started in the sport of running who you would like to encourage? Because this run is flat, scenic and can be easily shortened, you may find this a good one to share with them.

Dogs: Canine companions can be off-leash on the dyke but under control. Please keep them on-leash in mid to late April during the migration of shorebirds.

Of Interest: Since you are next to the Roberts Bank coal port jetty, did you know that this is the busiest single coal export terminal in

TOP: *Views along Brunswick Point in the fall*
(PHOTO COURTESY OF CHRISTINE GAIO)
BOTTOM: *The wide, flat, gravel trail along Brunswick Point*

North America and that it ships over 20 million tonnes of coal a year? This, of course, is burned in other countries and doesn't affect British Columbia's CO_2 emission levels, only the export country's balance sheet and, well, the planet's too.

You are at the terminus of the Fraser River, which starts 1375 km northeast in Mount Robson Provincial Park. Have you ever heard of the Berg Lake hike at Mount Robson? It's one of British Columbia's classic hikes and, I suggest, one for your bucket list.

As you run, you are on the edge of Tsawwassen First Nations land. They are one of the few BC First Nations bands to have settled land claims. Currently, the Tsawwassen Nation has a 1.2-million-square-foot megamall, slated to open in 2016, just east of the end of your run.

Eco-Insight: Shorebird Migration

April is the apex of spring. Tree leaves are budding, hummingbirds feed on native flowers and warblers return from their Central American habitats. But hummingbirds are hard to spot, and warblers flitter about high in the trees. So what is happening that's easy to see? If you head to Brunswick Point or Boundary Bay in April at high tide, you'll see shorebirds touch down on their northern migration – by the hundreds of thousands! Each "touch down" is a key feeding spot on the West Coast. Here, the shorebirds, which include sandpipers and dunlin, feed on a millimetre-thick, nutrient-rich slime – a biofilm of bacteria and diatoms. This "divine slime" happens to be found only in three areas of the Fraser River estuary, and only here in the mudflats north of Roberts Bank is it large enough to feed such huge numbers of shorebirds. Without this energy-enriched slime, the shorebirds might have difficulty finding the strength to complete their migrations.

It's important to note that most of these birds do not call this area home. The Arctic is their primary breeding ground and their winter home may be in Mexico. There, high-tech horticulture with drip irrigation, automated pesticide controllers, raised beds and large quantities of fertilizers empty into coastal mudflats similar to this one and compromise the wetlands. In other areas, thousands of more hectares are destroyed in the creation of shrimp farms. *We* benefit through imported fresh tomatoes, peppers and cucumbers in the winter, and

Migrating sandpipers are easily seen from Brunswick Point in spring and fall. Go at high tide. (PHOTO COURTESY OF ROB ALEXANDER)

inexpensive frozen shrimp year-round – but the shorebirds pay the externalized costs. It is important to recognize these interrelationships in today's global society in order to understand how economics and biodiversity concerns are linked.

Other Area Interests

If you wish to extend your time in the area, then you may wish to look into the Ladner Village Market, which runs every other Saturday in the summer. Alternatively, visit BC's most famous birding location – the George C. Reifel Migratory Bird Sanctuary on Westham Island, where, if you are lucky, you may see a sandhill crane or two.

Minnekhada Regional Park Loop

Distance: 5 – 10 km
Time: 35 min. – 2 hrs.
Level: moderate
Grade: moderate < 75 m
Public Transit Routes: no transit (see Notes)
Surface: dirt, gravel and rock

Activity Highlight

A good run has options. If you're feeling strong, then a hill climb might be in order. If the knees are sore, then soft ground is nice. If some mental stimulation is required, then a trail that flows around trees, rocky outcrops and across marsh bridges is a good bet. Minnekhada offers a multitude of variations depending on your motivation and mood. Choose your route, bring a map and get set to move those feet in this regional park gem.

Directions

Although there are several entrances to this park, the Minnekhada Lodge parking area is a good place to begin your run. Here you can choose your direction. If you choose clockwise, then the turnoff to the high knoll will come later in your run and you can choose to take the detour and climb, if you still have the energy. If you extend your run/hike to both knolls in the park, then expect about a 10-km activity with a 180-m elevation gain (and a great view from the high knoll). A shorter, moderate run is to run the main loop (Fern – Quarry – Log Walk – Lodge trails), with a side jaunt to the low knoll, for a total of a 5-km loop.

Notes

Transit & Transportation: Buses go to Coquitlam Station where you can find bus C38, which will take you to Cedar Drive and Chelsea Avenue. From here, you will have to walk or ride a bike the additional 4 km to access the park.

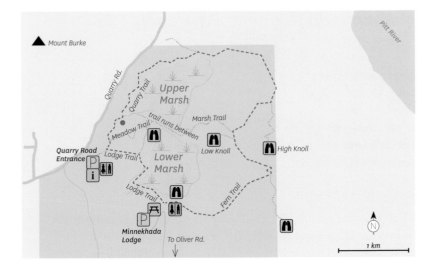

Maps: You can access maps of the trails online or free at Metro Vancouver Parks.

Restrooms: These are available at the Minnekhada Lodge parking area and at the Quarry Road (west side) entrance.

Timing: Any time of year is good for this park, though winter is muddier. If you would like to see inside the lodge, it's only open to the public on the first Sunday of each month, so plan accordingly.

Dogs: Your best friend should be on-leash while on all park trails.

Of Interest: Minnekhada means "beside running water" – derived from the Sioux language and applied by an early owner of the land who came from Minnesota – Sioux territory.

The lodge is rentable, so sometimes weddings fill the parking lot. This may mean you will have to park at the Quarry Road entrance to the west.

The lodge, formerly owned by two of BC's Lieutenant Governors at different times, has hosted royalty, including Princess Elizabeth.

If you take in the high knoll, pack a picnic snack, take a break and enjoy the panoramic view of Pitt River and beyond!

Historic Minnekhada Lodge

Eco-Insight: Rivers as Ribbons of Life

Rivers are conduits for nutrients, creators of new landscapes, transportation networks for countless species and ribbons of life that provide essential habitat. The Pitt River has influenced the Minnekhada landscape. It provides habitat for salmonid species, a recreational mecca for river kayakers and a conduit for resources from Pitt Lake. Historically, rivers were the natural arteries that attracted human settlement to the West. As critical components of the hydrological cycle, they drain approximately 75 per cent of the earth's land surface.

Consider one possible food web that begins in the Pitt River and extends outward: salmon fry feed on zooplankton (small or microscopic animals floating in the water) and the underwater larvae of insects. The fry's parents died on this river last fall and the nutrients from their decaying bodies are feeding mature insects about to lay eggs. Bears and eagles leave the forest to feed on dead salmon, while kingfishers and dippers feed on the fry. Trees that line the river absorb the fertilizing nutrients from salmon left on the ground by bears and

In summer, watch for dragonflies feeding over the marsh.
(PHOTO COURTESY OF ROB ALEXANDER)

other scavengers. The trees grow faster, stronger and taller, providing additional shade, which, in turn, keeps the water cooler (and more oxygenated) for the salmon. Squirrels feed on the many cones produced by the healthier trees, and, if unlucky, are predated by hawks. The hawks defecate in the forest, fungus begins to grow from this and banana slugs feed on the fungus. The slugs spread fungal spores and the resulting fungus helps create new soil for the trees that line the ribbon of life known as the river.

Other Area Interests

This geographic area of the Tri-Cities (Coquitlam, Port Moody and Port Coquitlam) includes an extensive dyke system that is great for runs and cycling. If you extend your time in this area, check out the Pitt River dyke for wide-open vistas of the mountains and valleys.

Lynn Loop at Lynn Headwaters Regional Park

Distance: 5 km
Time: 45 min. – 1.5 hrs.
Level: moderate
Grade: moderate < 175 m
Public Transit Route: 228 (see Notes)
Surface: gravel and dirt

Activity Highlight

Although this is a popular run for the North Shore crowd, it is still rare that I see many people on it, especially on weekdays. This is a quintessential temperate forest run, complete with rushing river, green shrubbery and tall, West Coast trees. The trail undulates around nurse logs and provides long, straight, dirt corridors only broken by roots

Start your run at Mills House; the outhouses are just behind.

(PHOTO COURTESY OF TREVOR BONAS)

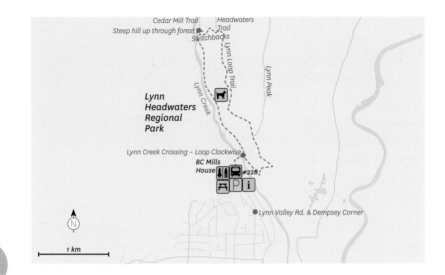

crisscrossing the trail. If you keep alert, it is unlikely you will miss the logging history of this area with its abundant artifacts, springboard-notched stumps and corduroy roads (more information on these terms is located in the Eco-Insight, Historic Logging on the North Shore on page 228).

Directions

From the Lynn Headwaters parking area, walk over the bridge and stay left on the trail along Lynn Creek. If you run clockwise in this direction, there are switchbacks that will take you uphill through the forest. Almost all of the trail's elevation gain is at these switchbacks and runners often prefer this direction.

Notes

Transit & Transportation: Buses go to the edge of the park. From the corner of Dempsey and Lynn Valley Road, you can run or walk the Varley trail 1.5 km to the trailhead. This trail runs parallel to the road.

Maps: These can be found online or free at Metro Vancouver Parks. Ask for the Lynn Headwaters Regional Park map.

Restrooms: These are located at the Lynn Headwaters entrance near the parking area.

Safety: Have you read the Safety & Security Planning section of this book yet? If not, be aware that although this is a small park, it is possible to get lost, so come prepared.

Timing: All year, but be aware that the upper area of this run can be very wet or have some snow in winter months.

Dogs: Furry friends should be on-leash while on all park trails.

Of Interest: Watch for logging artifacts en route including cables, tin cans, old wooden water pipes and other pieces of metal that have survived since the early 1900s. Leave what you find in its place.

Eco-Insight: Temperate Forests

Lynn Valley likely harboured the tallest trees in Canada before the logging of this area in the 19th century. Although there are still a few massive giants of Douglas fir, western hemlock, western red cedar and Sitka spruce in the area, most of the large trees that existed on the North Shore Mountains are now found only in pictures at the North Vancouver Archives. When you consider the locations on this planet where the right mix of moisture, nutrients and temperature combine to create some of the tallest trees on earth, Lynn Valley is one of those places. At the turn of the 20th century, this area contained springboards, crosscut saws, steam donkeys, flume lines, skid or corduroy logging roads and loggers to run them all (see Eco-Insight: Historic Logging on the North Shore on page 228). Some trees were so large they required splitting with dynamite – a woeful end for trees that may have sprouted during the zenith of the Roman Empire. How and when did these giants get here?

At the end of the Wisconsin Ice Age, about 11,000 years ago, British Columbia's climate completed its shift from subarctic to temperate. Pollen records from mud and ice cores show that lodgepole pine was the first of the conifer trees to populate this newly exposed landscape. Thousands of years later came the Douglas fir and Sitka spruce, and then, about 4,000 years ago, western hemlock and western red cedar arrived. An ancient ecosystem? Perhaps it's how you look at it. Some

The largest leaves you will see in the forest are of the skunk cabbage.

trees can live for 1,500 years. Relatively speaking, you could argue that Lynn Valley has a relatively new ecosystem here. It is anticipated that in just 50 years our climate will be two degrees Celsius warmer than it is today. With such a change in living conditions, I wonder what another 4,000 years beyond that will bring to this forest's biodiversity and balance.

Other Area Interests

The Lynn Canyon suspension bridge and ecology centre make up a well-known North Vancouver attraction. If you want to extend your day, pay a visit to Lynn Canyon and ask how to locate the trail to the blue pools for a cool dip in Lynn Creek after your run.

Go Further: Crippen Regional Park Loop on Bowen Island

Distance: 9 km
Time: 1 – 1.5 hrs.
Level: easy
Grade: moderate < 100 m
Public Transit Routes: 250, 257 to Horseshoe Bay, BC Ferries (Snug Cove-Horseshoe Bay), then C10, C11 on the island (see Notes)
Surface: gravel/dirt, bark and boardwalk

Activity Highlight

As close to rural as any activity in this book, Bowen Island is both a trail run and a day trip. Let's face it, to do this run probably means considering parking or transport to Horseshoe Bay, scheduled times for the ferry and the costs associated with each of these. Therefore, this trail run has to be worth it. It is! The feel as you step off the ferry is entirely different – relaxed, peaceful and easy-going. This vibe may not do anything for your speed workout, but consider this one part vacation and one part cardiovascular exercise.

Directions

The 1.6-km path from the ferry terminal to Killarney Lake begins next to the Bowen Island library. Walk up to Miller Road, turn right and follow it about 100 metres, then cross it and look for the Alder Grove trail to continue to the lake. When you reach the lake trail, go right (counter-clockwise) and watch for a good stop for a break at the north end of the boardwalk. The perimeter of the lake is 4 km. If you run this as a loop, you can take in the small hatchery as well.

Notes

Transit & Transportation: BC Ferries has 15 – 16 trips a day to Bowen Island, with the first ferry leaving Horseshoe Bay at 6:05 am. The 2014 return fare is between $12 for an adult fare (the fare may vary with

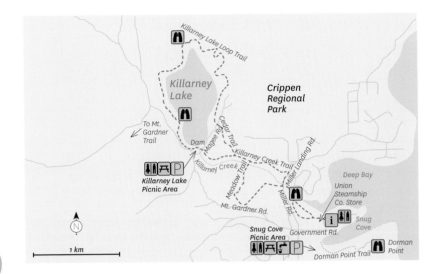

the season), while bicycles are a toonie. Leave your car on the West Vancouver side at the Lions parking, which is less expensive on weekends (and free on weekdays) than parking at BC Ferries. Bring your bike if you wish to explore further, or use the local transit system with schedules available from TransLink.

Maps: Trail maps can be found online or free at Metro Vancouver Parks.

Restrooms: These are located in Snug Cove at the start, and at the Killarney Lake picnic area.

Safety: Be aware you may be sharing the trails with cyclists, dog walkers and horseback riders.

Timing: Bowen Island has its annual Bowfest festival at the end of August for those interested in a community event tied to your activity. All seasons are delightful on Bowen Island, but spring and fall are especially beautiful.

Company: This activity is also a great walk with active older adults and makes a great day outing to share with them.

Dogs: Canine companions should be on-leash while on all park trails, but Bowen Islanders often are amenable to dogs being off-leash on the

TOP: *A colonnade of deciduous trees provides your lateral border throughout many parts of this run.* (PHOTO COURTESY OF JENN DICKIE)
BOTTOM: *A snack at the halfway mark: the far end of Killarney Lake*

island. There are several acceptable areas to run your dog off-leash. Ask around town when you get off the ferry if you wish to know more.

Of Interest: Much of this park was formerly an island resort with 180 cottages owned by the Union Steamship Company. The era of the dance pavilion, vaudeville shows and corporate parties ended in the 1940s, but the remnants remain to the watchful observer.

Killarney Lake is shallow with a dam at one end. Notice the drowned forest at the far end, a clue to the change in water level. This lake was formerly a drinking water supply for islanders.

Plan a lunch around this activity and spend your lunch money in the quaint ferry-terminal community of Snug Cove.

Eco-Insight: Wildlife Trees

While on your trail run, notice the homes you pass – wildlife homes, that is. The path from Snug Cove to Killarney Lake offers a superb locale to examine this key part of wildlife habitat. Look closely and you'll discover that understorey shrubs provide shelter for nesting birds, such as familiar robins and other thrushes, while the dead-standing wildlife trees provide a virtual condominium complex for other species. The condo strata members include great blue herons, bald eagles, osprey and various hawks, all of which nest on tree limbs, but I'd like to focus on the tree-cavity nesters, such as woodpeckers, owls, chickadees, ducks, swallows, salamanders, bats, squirrels and mice. The cavity nesters rely on woodpeckers to create the cavities, but each species, in turn, modifies it to fit its particular needs, with additional excavating, mud filling or lining of the cavities with moss, lichens, fungus, grasses and even insects (!) to suit. Watch for many dead-standing trees where the meadow trail crosses Killarney Creek and at the north end of Killarney Lake, rising straight out of the water.

Spring is peak time for nesting, so if you have an interest in a closer immersion with the habitat, listen for young chicks tweeting (the original "tweet") for first dibs on food as their parents forage for them. Watch for birds flying back to the trunks of trees rather than to the branches. Dead-standing wildlife trees contribute immensely to biodiversity in British Columbia, and the woodpeckers' cavities make it

LEFT: *Wildlife condo development*
RIGHT: *Watch for birds, such as this red-breasted sapsucker, that nest in the many dead-standing trees at the lake and en route to it.*
(PHOTOS COURTESY OF ROB ALEXANDER)

all possible. Do you have potential wildlife trees near your home? If so, consider ensuring that they remain as part of the habitat you share.

Other Area Interests

For a challenging hike on Bowen, you can attempt Mount Gardner. This is a 10-km, six-hour hike to Bowen's high point with panoramic views of Metro Vancouver, Howe Sound, the Sunshine Coast and Vancouver Island. For an extension to your Bowen Island day, a stop at West Vancouver's Whytecliff Park, just outside Horseshoe Bay, is a highlight for amazing sunsets, for watching scuba divers, for picnics or for just relaxing on the beach.

Hiking

"I have two doctors, my left leg, and my right."

—G.M. Trevelyan, English Historian, 1876 – 1972

Many Vancouverites grew up on classic hiking books such as Mary and David Macaree's *103 Hikes in Southwestern British Columbia* (1973) and *109 Walks in British Columbia's Lower Mainland* (1976), or Dougald MacDonald's *Hiking near Vancouver: Twenty Scenic Alpine Trails to Explore in B.C.'s Lower Mainland* (1971). Many have dog-eared the pages in the *Mountain Trail Guide for the South West Mainland Area of British Columbia* (1972), published by the Federation of Mountain Clubs of British Columbia. By the time my sons were walking, I was using Dawn Hanna's *Best Hikes and Walks of Southwestern British Columbia* (1997) to get out on the trails with them. My point with this short history is to say that Metro Vancouver has had, and continues to have, excellent hiking books outlining the region. In addition to the books, there are multiple websites and apps now available on the subject. You could fill each weekend with a different hike for many years to come. This chapter covers eight hikes that I consider a superb cross-section of what is available. It is an introduction designed to "hook you," turning hiking into a lifelong passion.

The North Shore Mountains form the backdrop for most of this chapter. If you followed the flight of a bald eagle from Horseshoe Bay to Deep Cove, you would pass over six of the seven hikes without much of a detour from side to side. Yet I can't help but think of them each as unique. Lighthouse Park has an ecology that resembles the Gulf Islands with its fire-scarred Douglas and grand firs. Sitting on the rocks at Point Atkinson in the park feels completely different from the Quarry Rock bluff on the east side of the North Shore overlooking Indian Arm. Capilano Canyon's river corridor is world-renowned and one of Vancouver's top tourism spots. Black Mountain via Cypress Bowl, while off the tourist track, is a climb to a fantastic view of Canada's third-largest city. Equally difficult to climb is the Stawamus Chief, but the view is completely different, overlooking

Intrepid hikers on a rainy day (PHOTO COURTESY OF SHELLEY FRICK)

Squamish and the blue fjord of Howe Sound. Both have a subalpine nature to them, but the Chief is unique with its lack of soil at the top of its climbable granite batholith. Whyte Lake and Cypress Falls round out this chapter with lesser-known features of the North Shore's environment – an off-the-circuit lake and a set of nearly hidden waterfalls.

Follow the Safety & Security Planning section in this book, along with the ten activity safety essentials, to prepare properly for your hiking. In fact, without looking, can you list the ten essentials to carry with you on a day hike? Good-quality, properly fit and well-broken-in hiking boots are a good investment. (Hiking shoes often don't offer sufficient ankle support.) Have a plan for your hike and know your limits and the limits of those hiking with you. It has been my observation that done properly, hiking can build muscles and body structure that will continue to support you well into your golden years. Just look around at the groups and organizations that get people together for hiking excursions. These clubs pull together a broad cross-section of society, with membership increasingly sustained by fit baby boomers who have a passion and motivation to keep their bodies in shape.

Be prepared that as your quads and calves strengthen with hiking, your head may tilt upwards. This will be due to your eyes continually looking skyward to higher peaks. If this happens, be sure to check out the current offerings of the Federation of Mountain Clubs of British Columbia or the Alpine Club of Canada. These organizations will surround you with a community of individuals who see BC's mountains as natural extensions to local urban trails. It isn't uncommon for a love of hiking to lead to mountaineering, hut-to-hut trekking, volkssporting, geocaching, orienteering and even to landscape photography, as well as search and rescue. It seems to me that what captures your attention controls your brain and, inevitably, your life.

Deep Cove's Quarry Rock & Indian Arm Lookout

Distance: 3.5 km
Time: 1.5 – 2 hrs.
Level: moderate (see Notes)
Grade: moderate < 150 m
Public Transit Routes: 211, 212, C15
Surface: dirt

Activity Highlight

Quarry Rock is a quick climb with a great view. It's simple to tuck it into a broader itinerary while on the North Shore. As hikes go, this is relatively easy, though it's classified as moderate as it is consistently up-hill (though most of the elevation gain is in the first kilometre). Since you can expect company at the rock outcrop overlooking Indian Arm, here's an idea. Make a point to talk to someone at the top; chances are good they are global visitors – this is a popular hike in the Vancouver guidebooks. Your conversation may shape how they view this region, while at the same time you may learn something new about another part of the world.

Directions

From the parking area at Panorama Park in Deep Cove, walk 0.25 km north on Panorama Drive to the trailhead on the left. The trail begins about ten metres up a shared driveway.

Notes

Maps: I suggest printing a map from a satellite photo off Google Maps, though you can also get maps from the District of North Vancouver for the Baden Powell Trail, of which this hike is a part.

Restrooms: These are located in Panorama Park in Deep Cove.

Safety: See note regarding dogs below.

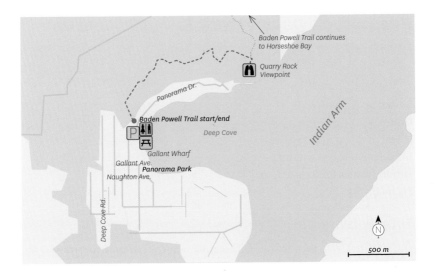

Timing: This is a good winter hike as it rarely has snow due to its relatively low elevation viewpoint and proximity to the ocean.

Company: I often find the climb to Quarry Rock seems to end before it begins when I'm immersed in an engaging conversation with my hiking partner. I think this trail speaks to reconnection. Call that long-lost friend you've been meaning to get in touch with and ask them to join you. Pack a snack and thermos and enjoy your view of, and over, the small boats on Indian Arm and of Belcarra and Buntzen ridge to the east.

This hike is also a great one to introduce young children to as it provides a challenge for them, gives a rewarding view but is short enough to hold their attention. Lastly, this is also a good first date hike if you know the other person is active but you don't know how much!

Dogs: Your best friend can be off-leash on this trail but under control at all times. Be cautious at the Quarry Rock viewpoint. In the past, dogs have become stranded on the rocks while trying to climb down to other rocks below.

Of Interest: There are very picturesque bridges over forest streams on this trail, so don't just bring your camera for a view from the top. Bring it for the journey.

TOP: *The view from the top looking toward Belcarra and Burnaby Mountain* (PHOTO COURTESY OF JACQUELINE SLAGLE)

BOTTOM: *Take time to appreciate the streams in this lush temperate forest.*

Due to its proximity to Vancouver, and how well known it is locally, this trail can be quite busy on summer weekends.

This trail is the start, or the end, depending on your direction, of the famous 42-km Baden Powell Trail that crosses the North Shore Mountains between Horseshoe Bay and Deep Cove. Every year athletes run the "Knee Knacker" from one end of the trail to the other (ending in Deep Cove).

Eco-Insight: Mycorrhizal Connections

Micro what, you ask? Pay attention to the soil below your feet on this hike. Below you are root systems, 90 per cent of which spread laterally out from a tree, often no deeper than 20 centimetres. These roots supply the tree with nutrients and water, but they don't do it alone. The roots have a close relationship with fungus underground (called *mycorrhizae*, meaning "fungus-root"). In fact, most species of plants have fungal partners, without which they could not grow. Douglas fir trees in this forest may have relationships with 2,000 different types of fungi, and dozens are connected just to their roots! How?

The mycorrhizae fungus extends the nutrient-gathering area with its *hyphae* (a branching structure of filaments) to collect water and nutrients, especially phosphorous and nitrogen, for the tree roots. In turn, the tree delivers something to the fungus that the fungus cannot provide for itself – sugars from photosynthesis. The fungus absorbs so much sugar it can expand to gigantic proportions underground. Tree growth, however, improves due to the extra nutrients and water supplied by the fungus. Effectively, the fungus allows the tree to extend its reach many times beyond itself, and the fungus is able to grow and reproduce without making its own food.

The reproductive fungal fruits, called truffles, are filled with spores and are eaten at night by animals such as the northern flying squirrel. When the squirrels eat the truffles, the spores pass through their digestive systems and are later defecated into another area of the forest, thereby expanding the range of the fungus. The web of life is wondrous!

Underground, these tree roots are connected my mycorrhizal fungi, which help support the lush growth of this forest.

(PHOTO COURTESY OF LORI GEOSITS)

Other Area Interests

If you have more time in Deep Cove after this short hike, then plan a side trip to either Cates Park to scope out a future picnic site or to Maplewood Flats for a birding excursion.

Capilano Canyon Regional Park Forest & River Loop

Distance: 6 km
Time: 2 – 3 hrs.
Level: moderate
Grade: moderate < 300 m
Public Transit Routes: 232, 236, 247
Surface: dirt

Activity Highlight

Capilano Canyon (or more specifically the suspension bridge over it) is one of Vancouver's top attractions. Therefore, you can expect a person or two (or a hundred) near you during this activity. However, like any trail, the farther you get from the start, the rarer the crowds. In fact, I suspect you will find areas in this 6-km loop that are positively serene. I've heard that 80 per cent of people use 20 per cent of any given area. I suggest these are the areas mostly around parking lots, and if I were to guess if that applies to Capilano Canyon, I'd put it at 90/10. The highlight for getting past the crowds is to be, peacefully, in one of Vancouver's top attractions.

Directions

Begin your hike from the parking area on the east side of Cleveland Dam. Cross the dam and go down the Lower Shingle Bolt trail until it intersects with the Capilano Pacific trail. Continue down the Capilano Pacific to the viewpoint over the river, then double back to the Lower Shingle Bolt and turn right. This will take you to the Pipeline trail and over Pipeline Bridge. Once over the bridge, take the Coho Loop trail up the canyon until the drop-off area for the hatchery. At the far side and to the right of the hatchery is the Palisades trail, which will take you back to your starting point. This total loop and spur to the viewpoint on the west side of the canyon is about 6 km long and is another good run. Note that side trails off this route take you to some of the

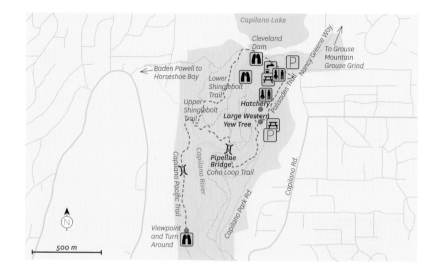

The view of the watershed while hiking over Cleveland Dam

(PHOTO COURTESY OF ROB ALEXANDER)

largest old-growth trees in Metro Vancouver. There are dozens of confusing intersecting trails in Capilano Canyon, so if you aren't familiar with the area, read the many signboards posted throughout the park and carry a Capilano Canyon map available from Metro Vancouver Parks.

Notes

Maps: Find maps for the trails online or free at Metro Vancouver Parks.

Restrooms: These are located at the start and at the hatchery bus loop, just before the Palisades trail.

Safety: Be extra careful around the gorge edges as they can be slippery and the drop is extreme.

Timing: This is a great temperate rainforest hike in winter.

Company: This hike is great with kids because you can shorten or lengthen the hike to suit your party. However, the trail has substantial drops (but it's well fenced) into Capilano Canyon, so be careful with kids. The fish hatchery and Cleveland Dam will also hold their interest.

Dogs: Furry friends should be on-leash while on all park trails.

Of Interest: The Cleveland Dam spillway is a stopping point before you even begin this hike. Capilano Reservoir is on your right. Do you know where your water comes from? If not, it may be from here – this is one of three reservoirs serving over two million people in Metro Vancouver. If you want to know more about the watersheds that supply you with fresh water from your tap, then join a free Capilano watershed tour from Metro Vancouver – surely one of the best deals in town and a great way to see a landscape not open to the public. Learn more about watersheds in the Eco-Insight on this topic on page 145.

At the hatchery entrance (in front of the tour bus turnaround), there is a near record-sized western yew tree (see Eco-Insight below). In fact, four out of the province's five biggest yews are here in Capilano Regional Park!

If you wish to see or learn more about Pacific salmon, pause at the hatchery and have a look at the displays.

TOP: *The view above your hike in Capilano Canyon is good too.*
BOTTOM: *Watch for mushrooms along the trail in the fall.*

(PHOTOS COURTESY OF TERRY BEREZAN)

Eco-Insight: Western Yew

The western yew is an enigmatic tree. Parts of the tree are toxic enough to produce cardiac arrest if ingested. Yet it also produced one of the greatest cancer treatment drugs of the 20th century – Taxol. Historically, logging companies considered yew trees waste wood and burned them at logging sites. In the mid-1980s, a compound extracted from its bark was found to shrink many cancerous tumours. Suddenly thrust into the spotlight, Taxol was a hot commodity in the 1990s. Approximately 700 kilograms of bark were required to make enough of the drug to treat one case of cancer. Because the yew tree is not common in British Columbia, it was a good news story when, in 1994, Taxol was ultimately synthesized in a lab. This is a classic story of the secrets held in biological diversity and is but one reason to ensure biodiversity remains paramount in decisions made in this province and worldwide. Do you know other medicines discovered in nature? Here's a list of a few:

- digitalis for heart medication from foxglove;
- morphine from the poppy;
- aspirin from willow bark;
- ACE inhibitors from the pit viper for high blood pressure; and
- AZT for treating HIV-AIDS from a marine sponge.

Globally, there are still many opportunities to "bioprospect," as only 10 – 15 per cent of plants have been investigated for their chemistry and biology (and just 0.1 per cent of microbes have been studied). However, many species, especially in the tropics, have tiny ranges and could be eliminated before we even know they exist, let alone study them.

Other Area Interests

If you are at Capilano Canyon and have never been up to Grouse Mountain, this may be your opportunity. The skyride is just up the hill from the start of this activity, as is the Grouse Grind that takes you to the same point on top but with more, um, shall we say, energy expenditure!

Lighthouse Park Forest & Ocean Edge Loop

Distance: 4 – 6 km
Time: 1.5 – 2.5 hrs.
Level: easy – moderate
Grade: moderate < 150 m
Public Transit Route: 250
Surface: dirt, gravel, rock

Activity Highlight

I find this park takes time to hike. The total mileage is low, but the time you take to explore can easily be half a day. Why? It's all the side trails to the ocean's edge. The west-facing Juniper Point and Shore Pine Point face Bowen Island and the entrance to Howe Sound; Point Atkinson and Starboat Cove look across to Stanley Park, downtown and West Point Grey, while the park summit provides a view beyond the 49th Parallel. With the addition of rock bluffs that seem to beguile you to stay seated on the ocean-facing granite, you may find your watch hands move faster than your feet.

Directions

The park entrance is easy to miss, because it is a small road off Marine Drive. Watch carefully for the wooded sign on the water side of Marine Drive. Once at the parking area, I suggest a counter-clockwise loop around the perimeter of the park. I highly recommend bringing a map since it is easy to get turned around in this park. Begin by taking the Juniper Loop to Juniper Point and around to the Shore Pine trail (trail names derive from the trees that dot the landscape at each point). Follow Shore Pine to the point and beyond to the lighthouse. Next to Lighthouse Point is a small building that has restrooms, and directly behind these is East Beach trail and a quaint secluded cove. Double back to the Valley trail, veer right to Arbutus trail, to Eagle Point, and then up to Summit trail. This is the high point of the park and is worth

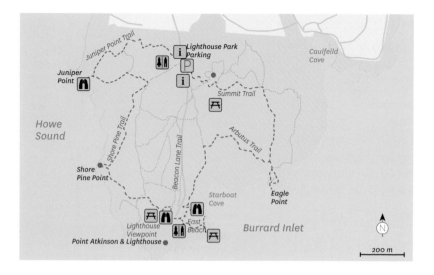

the time. Please be sure to stay on the trail, as the environment is fragile. An errant foot can tear multi-year moss growth off a rocky bluff and change its micro-environment drastically. From here, it is a quick walk back to the parking area. The Beacon Lane trail provides a quick way out of the park if required.

Notes

Maps: Find maps for the trails online or free at the West Vancouver Parks and Recreation website (westvancouver.ca/parks-recreation) or at the kiosk in the parking area.

Restrooms: These are located just to the west of the parking area and near the trailhead to the viewpoint at Point Atkinson.

Safety: Have you read the Safety & Security Planning section of this book yet? If not, be aware that although this is a small park, it's possible to get lost in it, so come prepared.

Timing: Any time of year is good for this hike, but I'd suggest a summer evening to take in the sunset at Starboat Cove or at the summit.

Company: East Beach trail to the cove is truly a place to experience a sunset, a picnic lunch or a date. Pick your company to suit!

Watch for bald eagles soaring overhead or sitting in the park's tall trees.
(PHOTO COURTESY OF RORRI MCBLANE)

Dogs: Lighthouse Park is one of West Vancouver's off-leash parks, although dogs should be under control at all times.

Of Interest: Lighthouse Park has numerous old-growth trees – while on the trails, watch for large Douglas firs. They will be the ones that have wide but straight bases, with deeply fluted folds in reddish orange bark. These trees will probably be black with scars from fires that happened between the mid-1800s to as recently as 1930. Built to withstand fire, these trees have a 15 – 30 cm thick shield of bark that surrounds their trunks. Watch for bald eagles perching atop these forest giants.

When you are at the lighthouse, you are also on the rocky bluffs of Point Atkinson. This is the main point used for marking the rise and

TOP: *Lighthouse Park is a perfect spot to enjoy a sunset.*

(PHOTO COURTESY OF ROB ALEXANDER)

BOTTOM: *The rocky shoreline that surrounds Lighthouse Park is a draw itself.*

fall of tides in our local tide tables. Many of the activities in this book (running at Locarno, canoeing at Widgeon Creek or kayaking out of Deep Cove), in fact, suggest to use tide tables measured from this location.

The first lighthouse, built here in 1874, had a steam-powered foghorn. The surrounding forest was saved as a source of fuel to power it.

The west-facing bluff at Juniper Point is an ideal place for a rock climb over the sea. There are many climbing cracks on the cliffs and most routes are top-roped with good bolts. Stop by to watch rock climbers on your hike, or perhaps consider a future activity of a local rock climb at this gorgeous site.

Do you have a piece of land that you frequent and are passionate about? People involved with the Lighthouse Park Preservation Society do and they are passionate about this park! The group works to protect the natural integrity of the park – it has a unique natural history and is highly vulnerable to urban pressures.

Eco-Insight: Tides

Do you know what causes the tides? Congratulations if you said gravitational forces between the earth and the moon. In fact, the world's oceans ebb and flow due to the balance between the gravitational and centrifugal forces of the earth, the moon and the earth-moon system, and even the sun. As the earth spins, oceans bulge toward the moon when they are facing the moon, due to its gravitational pull. However, oceans on the side of the earth opposite the moon also bulge (this time away from the moon but still away from the surface of the earth), because on the "far side" of the earth, the moon's gravitational pull is less than on the near side. The sun's gravitational pull also plays a role, causing high tides to be higher and low tides to be lower during full and new moons. Further complicating the process, in the time the earth completes one 24-hour rotation, the moon moves nearly an hour forward in its own orbit. If you pay attention to when the moon rises, you will notice it rises 50 minutes later each night, and that affects the tides too. (For a thorough explanation of tide-producing forces, take the time to search out a good educational website that includes diagrams and animations.)

Land masses disrupt the flow of ocean waters as they rush from high to low tides, and few places show that better than on the east side of Vancouver Island, specifically in the Strait of Georgia. The narrow gaps between land masses, variation in water depths, strong winds and the reflection of waves off islands make the strait's tides very complex and irregular. Tidal currents meet in Desolation Sound as they wrap around Vancouver Island, resulting in areas of very rough and powerful tidal surge. Surge areas are popular with river kayakers and thrill-seekers because of the large waves that exist within them.

Other Area Interests

Two other beautiful beach areas in West Vancouver are worth noting. Caulfeild Cove, just east of Lighthouse Park, is a small, local beach with limited parking but another charming place for a picnic. Whytecliff Park, west toward Horseshoe Bay, is larger, often filled with scuba divers and is always a good place for playing on the beach and exploring the rocky ground.

Cypress Mountain to Black Mountain Summit Hike

Distance: 6 km
Time: 4 hrs.
Level: difficult
Grade: difficult < 400 m
Public Transit Routes: no transit
Surface: dirt

Activity Highlight

In the winter of 2010, Black Mountain was off limits due to security for the Vancouver Olympics. For those of us who snowshoe, it was sorely missed. We were patient, as we knew this great winter snowshoe trail was also a fantastic summer hiking trail with mirror lakes reflecting a subalpine forest. If I were to choose a season to visit the mountain, it would certainly be fall, as the low shrubbery will be in its most striking reds and yellows. Mirrored in the lakes, the forests' colours are stunning!

Directions

There is no public transit to Cypress Bowl. However, if you choose to do this as a snowshoe in the winter, refer to the directions regarding a mountain bus shuttle to the trailhead for this activity. This information is located in the introduction to the snowshoeing section of this book. From the downhill ski area parking lot, obtain a backcountry pass (not required in the summer) at guest services and continue west, past the lodge and the Eagle Express chairlift on your left. After about 100 metres, there is a signpost leading you off the ski run onto a trail. There is a fork in the trail at 200 metres. Take the left-hand trail at the signpost and climb parallel to the ski run. The right-hand trail goes to Yew Lake and beyond to the 30-km Howe Sound Crest Trail – something for another day!

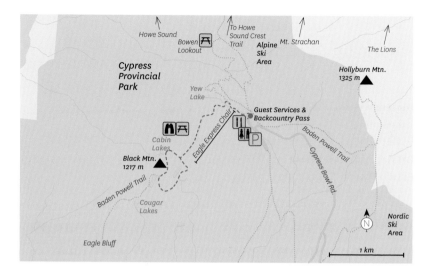

Notes

Maps: Maps for the trails are online at BC Parks (env.gov.bc.ca/bcparks) under Cypress Provincial Park.

Restrooms: These are only available at the lodge, at the start of this hike.

Safety: Have you read the Safety & Security Planning section of this book yet? If not, be aware that it is possible to get lost in the mountains, so come prepared.

Timing: This is a good hike year-round, but it becomes a snowshoe in the winter. Melting snow may make shoulder seasons mucky.

Company: This hike is challenging enough to get a young teenager not just gasping for air but also feeling a sense of pride and accomplishment after completing it. Do you know a teen who could use some outdoor time?

Dogs: Furry friends should be on-leash while on all BC park trails.

Of Interest: There are majestic views at the top Black Mountain after a continuous climb past subalpine lakes to the summit(s). There are two summits, with one looking north to Howe Sound, the Lions, Crown and Goat mountains, while the other looks west and south to Vancouver Island and downtown Vancouver.

TOP: *A picturesque lake not far from the high point of the hike*
BOTTOM: *Some hikes suit headlamps for your return as you can then experience sunset over Vancouver at the summit.*

(PHOTO COURTESY OF CAM ANDERSON)

The top of the trail can include a loop that takes you through mature forest toward Eagle Bluffs, around a couple of subalpine lakes and back out to the main trail next to the ski run.

Eco-Insight: Geology of Vancouver Island

From atop Black Mountain, look west to Vancouver Island and think about what you know about it. You probably know some major cities and towns, perhaps that its vegetation differs and certainly that its rainfall is less (at least on the eastern, rain shadow side) than in Metro Vancouver. Perhaps you know of certain animals that are more prevalent there, or of others that are completely absent, as compared to BC's coastal mainland. You certainly know it's not cheap to get there on BC Ferries! However, did you know that, geologically speaking, it is worlds apart from what is under your feet on Black Mountain?

Most of British Columbia is composed of island chains (referred to as *terranes*, pieces of the earth's crust formed elsewhere) that have been pushed by continental drift, combined with plate tectonics, toward and into the continent of North America over the last 200 million years. Think of the process as a slow-motion conveyor belt moving land that used to be out in the Pacific toward North America's beaches, which once ended at present-day Calgary and Dawson Creek. For a visual representation of these stacked terranes, look at a map of British Columbia and notice its northwest-southeast-oriented mountain ranges between the Rockies and the Coastal Mountains. Contrary to appearances, Vancouver Island isn't a terrane that has broken away from the mainland; rather, the conveyor belt just hasn't brought it completely to the shores of North America yet. Vancouver Island, along with the Gulf Islands, Haida Gwaii and everything west of California's San Andreas Fault, is sliding northeast and will collide with northwestern BC and coastal Alaska in 50 million years or so. The proof comes from the island's fossil record, which contains species similar to those found in Asia but substantially different from other fossils found on mainland BC.

The grey jay is a common visitor to subalpine environments.

(PHOTO COURTESY OF ROB ALEXANDER)

Other Area Interests

The West Vancouver Seawall and Ambleside Park are great extensions to this day to add some beach time to your subalpine hike. If it is summer, consider the week-long Harmony Arts Festival at Ambleside Park in early August as an extension.

Whyte Lake in West Vancouver

Distance: 6 km
Time: 1.5 – 2 hrs.
Level: moderate
Grade: moderate < 250 m
Public Transit Route: 250
Surface: gravel, dirt, pavement

Activity Highlight

Many locals don't realize there are two lakes tucked into the hillside below Cypress Mountain between the Upper Levels Highway (Highway 1) and the Sea-to-Sky Highway. Do an Internet map search for West Vancouver and you will see both Eagle and Whyte lakes. Unless you're a local, I'd guess that you have never been to either. However, with both the Trans Canada and the Baden Powell trails being part of the Whyte Lake hike, it is likely to become increasingly popular. Upon starting this hike, be sure to take time along the Trans Canada for a leisurely start that overlooks Fisherman's Cove Marina.

Directions

Begin at the Gleneagles Community Centre, walking toward Vancouver on the north side of Marine Drive. This turns into Seaview Walk, part of the Trans Canada Trail system, and a charming start to this trail. Follow this above both Marine Drive and past the viewpoint looking down to Fisherman's Cove Marina. You will see a chain-link fence blocking access to the railway and tunnel. Here you diverge north on a path uphill, over the tunnel and through a mature forest. For a small portion, you will be walking on a section of the original Highway 99. Notice plants reclaiming the old road as they grow through cracks in the pavement. Watch for a sign on your left that says "Whyte Lake." Just before a large, green, water tank turn right up the trail along Whyte Creek, staying left at the fork (not continuing on the Trans Canada Trail) and along a pleasant trail that will take you to a 300-m boardwalk and to this jewel of a lake. Plan this hike as a loop

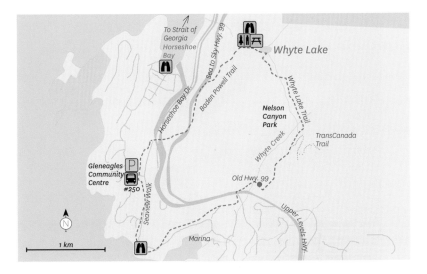

and when you leave the lake, head west past the outhouse to the Baden Powell (BP) Trail. Go left on the BP until it takes you to a trailhead parking area and Horseshoe Bay Drive. Here you cross under the new Highway 1 and walk for about 100 m along the old Highway 1 to cross (at a crosswalk to your right) and return to your starting point. Please be extremely aware of your safety and traffic at this point, as motorists will not expect people on the highway.

Notes

Maps: Beyond the map in this book, I suggest printing a map from a satellite photo off Google Maps or searching for the Nelson Canyon/ Gleneagles trails area.

Restrooms: These are located at Gleneagles Community Centre and at Whyte Lake itself. In fact, if I had to vote on the best-looking outhouse on the North Shore, the Whyte Lake outhouse would be a contender. Drink some extra water on the trail to have an excuse to visit it!

Company: Once when I visited this lake, I noticed someone left a foot-long, popsicle-stick-built boat that they must have launched off the dock. It made me wonder if it was a child's project. It also made me realize that this could be a good place to take active children.

TOP: *Watch for trilliums on the trail in May.*
BOTTOM: *Temperate forests are abundant in Metro Vancouver.*

(PHOTOS COURTESY OF ROB ALEXANDER)

Dogs: Your best friend should be on-leash while on the Whyte Lake trail as this is an environmentally sensitive area.

Of Interest: Whyte Lake is swimmable in the summer and has a dock suitable for jumping into the water.

If you have hiked Quarry Rock in Deep Cove, that is one end of the 42-km-long Baden Powell Trail. This hike is at the opposite end.

Eco-Insight: Sea Fog & Temperate Forests

The North Shore Mountains are the barrier between the moist marine air and the dryer interior air. As air moves across the Strait of Georgia, it accumulates moisture. When the air mass encounters the mountains, it must inevitably rise. As it does, it cools. The cooler air's capacity to hold moisture decreases and may, at some point, no longer be able to carry its moisture. If not, it could condense in pockets like that over Whyte Lake, creating fog, drizzle or precipitation.

Here the trees protect steep valleys from wind, allowing cold air to sink into stream drainages. The forest itself creates its own microclimate, making the air feel warmer or cooler than the surrounding areas. In the winter, the dark canopy absorbs the sun's rays and reradiates some heat downward to the insulated vegetation below, while in the summer the shade and transpiration of water from conifer needles has a cooling effect. Throughout the year, rain is often absorbed in the canopy when fog condenses on the needles.

Trees suck huge volumes of water in the ground into their roots and transpire it through their needles into the air. The theory on how trees pull water up is that evaporation from the needles creates a vacuum behind it and the vacuum draws the water up. It may take only 36 hours to transport water 100 m from roots to canopy. Over the course of a day, a mature tree can draw up vast quantities of water. All this temperature and water action determines what survives and, ultimately, which plants, insects, amphibians, birds and mammals call this home.

Other Area Interests

For a longer hike and overview of this area, pair this hike with the next one listed in the book to Cypress Falls, another jewel in West

Vancouver (the total distance for both hikes is 9 km). It is worth looking into Sewell's Marina at Horseshoe Bay for both its history and its boats and tours offered. If you have never rented a boat to explore in, you can do this at Sewell's – perhaps a future adventure. If you are driving, the scenic route along Marine Drive back toward the Lions Gate Bridge is a worthwhile return to Vancouver.

Cypress Falls Temperate Forest Hike

Distance: 3 km
Time: 1 – 1.5 hrs.
Level: easy
Grade: minimal < 110 m
Public Transit Routes: 253, C12 (see Notes)
Surface: dirt

Activity Highlight

This short but great winter hike takes you through a dense forest of old-growth western red cedar, western hemlock and Douglas fir. This moss-draped trail through moist, temperate forest is quintessential West Coast and leads to two waterfalls. Many trees in this forest are 300 – 400 years old, a remnant of what the North Shore used to have from Deep Cove to Horseshoe Bay. The falls are nice, but I think the highlight of this hike is the old-growth trees that you pass along the way.

Directions

Take Exit #4 off the Upper Levels Highway and stay right on Woodgreen Drive in West Vancouver. Follow the road to Woodgreen Place and begin your hike near the tennis courts. The forest trail is at the far end of the lot. This area has many meandering trails and has few signs, but begin by going left and uphill. As a general rule, keep the sound of the creek on your right and climb uphill on the trails that appear most well-trodden. Stay left at the first junction and watch for a viewpoint of the Lower Cypress Falls from a rocky outcrop above the canyon (about ten minutes in). Don't cross the bridge but instead continue uphill to the upper falls. Just prior to the bridge, turn left and climb uphill past old-growth trees for about 500 metres. You will reach a road where just beyond is the viewpoint for the upper waterfall cascading into the canyon. From here, you can walk across the Cypress Creek bridge on the road. You are now on the other side of the creek. Watch for a trail back into the forest after about 200 m that will return you to the lower

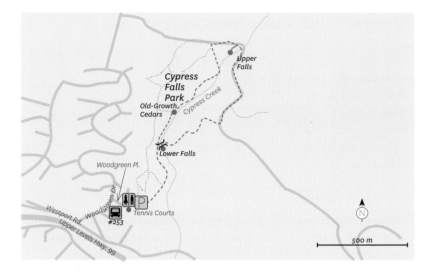

falls via the wooded bridge you saw earlier. Again, there is a network of minor trails extending in multiple directions from the lower falls but only two primary trails – stay on the well-trodden paths and it should be easy to locate both fall viewpoints. Hike among giant trees and just enjoy your time exploring this wonderful area of the North Shore. If you follow this in a clockwise direction to the upper falls, you should locate it in about 30 – 40 minutes.

Notes

Transit & Transportation: Get off bus #253 at Woodgreen Drive to access the park. Follow the road uphill and turn right onto Woodgreen Place. Follow it to the entrance of Cypress Falls. Finding the park can be a challenge because it isn't well signed.

Maps: The North Shore Trail Map 1:20,000, available at Mountain Equipment Co-op, is the best map for this area.

Restrooms: These are not available at this site, a shame because of all that running water!

Safety: Some of the side trails run dangerously close to the edge of the canyon. With moist, mossy-covered rocks, it would be easy to slip off the edge and into the canyon below, so be aware.

TOP: *Cypress Falls*
BOTTOM: *Hiking through the old-growth forest at Cypress Falls*

(PHOTOS COURTESY OF ROB ALEXANDER)

Timing: This is a great rainy-day hike in a Gore-Tex jacket. Go in the off-season as the falls are at their peak flow and the rainforest is at its most majestic.

Dogs: Canines can be off-leash but under control as Cypress Falls is a dog-friendly park, but as stated in the safety section above, be aware of the canyon edges.

Of Interest: For a longer hike and overview of this area, pair this hike with the one to Whyte Lake, another jewel in West Vancouver.

Eco-Insight: Western Red Cedar

Does any tree represent coastal British Columbia more completely than western red cedar? It is immortalized in ancient totems, it shelters many homes with roof shingles and it is ubiquitous along almost every trail we walk throughout the coast. Red cedar is listed among the oldest trees known in the province (there are individual red cedars as old as 2,000 years). Its fragrant aroma is known to most, almost from birth, and its stringy bark, buttress trunk and dark-green scale-like "leaves" make it possibly the most recognizable conifer. The biggest beams in any First Nation longhouse are cedar, carved masks in Gastown tourist shops are cedar and the chest in your grandmother's attic? Yes, that's likely cedar too. This tree connects us spatially in time to another era of dugout canoes, bentwood boxes, cedar clothing, dye and even sewing fiber. Centuries-old living trees show scars of plank or bark removal from a time before written language. Anthropologists call these CMTs: culturally modified trees. Is it any wonder this tree is so revered?

Based on studies of pollen found in glacier ice cores, trees in general slowly re-established themselves throughout British Columbia after the last ice age retreated about 11,000 years ago. Red cedar, the final conifer to establish itself, arrived in some areas 4,000 years ago and in other areas as recently as only 2,000 years ago. Take a moment to do the math on their age and their comparatively recent re-establishment in our forests: the old-growth red cedars you find at Cypress Falls could be as young as second or third generation! Climate warming, however, is increasing their mortality and Dr. Lori Daniels, a biogeographer at the University of British Columbia, believes water stress

There are still a number of places on the North Shore to find giant western red cedars. The trail to Cypress Falls is one of those locations.

(PHOTO COURTESY OF KIM MCLEOD)

in trees will change our forests dramatically. She says future forests are expected to be sparser and more vulnerable to insects and disease.

Other Area Interests

As suggested above, you can easily pair this with the Whyte Lake hike. For an added urban adventure, go for a walk through Dundarave Village in West Vancouver and the west end of the sea walk to John Lawson Park.

Go Further: Stawamus Chief South Summit Challenge in Squamish

Distance: 4 km
Time: 2.5 – 3.5 hrs.
Level: difficult
Grade: difficult < 550 m
Public Transit Routes: no transit
Surface: dirt, rock, gravel

Activity Highlight

Stawamus Chief is the second-largest granite dome in the world. The area directly around "the Chief" is among the most popular areas in North America for rock climbing and bouldering. From the pullout off Highway 99, you should be able to see climbers on the face of the Chief itself (in summer). These tiny, colourful dots on the face may be climbing their way to the top. I promise this activity follows a gentler (but it's all relative isn't it?) slope!

Directions

From the parking area of Stawamus Chief Provincial Park, follow the wide path south past the camping area and outhouses to the trail that climbs to the left. The ascent is steep and begins with stairs. Take the side trail to the bridge very near the start for a view over Howe Sound and a look at the creek you will be following on most of your hike to the summit. If you were to continue over the bridge and along this southerly trail, it would take you to Shannon Falls in 1.5 km. For now, though, retrace your steps back to the trail, continue uphill to the junction and stay left to access First Peak/South Summit (the right fork takes you to the Second and Third peaks for an 11-km hike in total).

Notes

Maps: You can find maps for the Chief trails online (env.gov.bc.ca/bcparks) under Stawamus Chief Provincial Park.

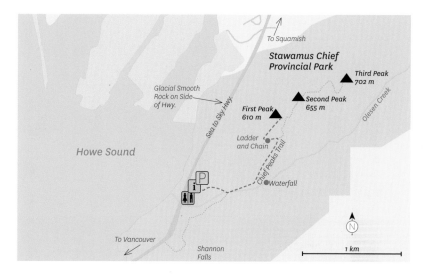

Restrooms: These are available at the start of the trail in the camping area only. There are no restrooms at the summit.

Safety: As you near the summit of this trail, you will be hiking on the granite outcrop itself. This hike is a little more technical, hence the "challenge" in the activity title. There is a ladder and a 10-m rope line that will help you with your footing on the rock. It's at this point along the trail that dogs are often unable to continue. In addition, the rock surface itself can be slippery when wet or frosty, so take extra caution when leaving the trail for the rock surface (see Timing below). This hike is for more seasoned hikers or intermediate hikers wishing to challenge themselves a little. The view from the top over Howe Sound and the Sunshine Coast is stunning, but be careful to stay back from the edge as it drops off quickly.

Timing: Spring through fall is the best time for this hike, as frost, snow and ice make the rock surfaces very slippery and potentially dangerous. Clear days will offer the best views north to Garibaldi Provincial Park, west to the Sunshine Coast and southwest to Vancouver Island.

Company: Do you know a teenager who could use both some outside time and a challenge? If so, bring them along for this hike and then stop at the Squamish Adventure Centre to show them the other

TOP: *Standing atop the Chief*
BOTTOM: *The Chief from the Squamish Estuary*

extreme sports Squamish is famous for – kiteboarding, rock climbing, mountain biking and river kayaking to name a few.

Dogs: Furry pals must be on-leash in this park. Be aware there are several sections with steep inclines, sudden drop-offs and narrow ledges that can pose a danger. The ladder section is a common turn-around point for dogs. The trail to the Central and North peaks does not allow dogs.

Of Interest: The Chief provides good nesting habitat for the peregrine falcon (they nest from March to July). If you watch closely from the parking area, you may see one flying near the face of the rock or heading out over the estuary for a meal.

Watch for a pullout on the west side of Highway 99 across from the park. There you can see what past glacial action has done to the rock surface. A beautiful smooth and curved surface with striations (grooves in the rock) is now visible due to the expansion of Highway 99 in 2009. It is worth seeing and rubbing your hand over it if you have never seen, close up, the power of glacial action.

This trail is very busy, especially on summer weekends. There are fewer crowds in the mornings and on weekdays.

Eco-Insight: Granite Batholith

The Stawamus Chief, a 700-metre granite dome with numerous vertical cliffs, is an excellent rock climbing site. This massive granite batholith formed about 100 million years ago by the slow cooling and solidification of a huge body of molten rock (magma) deep inside the earth's interior. A combination of upward movement and surface erosion helped this immense rock outcrop become the dominant structure on the surrounding landscape. More recently, glacial erosion has softened its edges, polished its surface and shaped its steep walls. While resting at the summit, look for glacial striations (lines scratched into the rock by glaciers moving over the granite) and consider the ecological conditions set up since the last glaciers retreated about 11,000 years ago.

Immediately after glacial retreat, minerals in the rock began weathering and creating mineral soil. Meanwhile, wind, water and animals transported pollen, spores and seeds from bordering ice-free areas. The new nutrient-rich soil provided a base to support growth. Mineral-seeking plants grew, died and decomposed, creating organic matter. This organic soil supported different vegetation more suited to these new conditions. Today, the combination of the mineral and organic soil forms the foundation of our coastal forest. Its depth relates to the amount of erosion, weathering and decomposition that have occurred since the last ice age. The soil depth at the bottom of the trail is probably less than a metre thick, while harsher conditions at the summit have kept it from accumulating. Imagine yourself as a 75-metre tall, organic-soil-loving tree. How deep would you put your roots? Well, here deep is not an option, so watch out for those Squamish winds.

Other Area Interests

A great extension to this hike is a side trip to Shannon Falls (a 3-km return trip from the bridge near the start of the trail). In the greater area, the Squamish estuary and training dyke are also excellent extensions to this day. Birds, kiteboarders and views back to the Stawamus Chief abound. Visit the Squamish Adventure Centre on Highway 99 for directions and a map of the area.

Active kids can climb the Chief too! (PHOTO COURTESY OF JEN REILLY)

Snowshoeing

"Snow provokes responses that reach right back to childhood."

—Andy Goldsworthy, British Artist, 1956 –

If you were to look at upward trends in outdoor activities, snowshoeing would stand out. Lighter and more dynamic equipment may be why the sport is becoming a substantial part of winter recreation in Metro Vancouver. Though the city gets short shrift when it comes to its winter rainy season, those "in the know" move to higher elevations where wet turns to white. For the most part, the peaks of the North Shore Mountains are six degrees Celsius cooler than the airport temperature. Knowing this, you can predict that rainy winter days where the mercury falls below six degrees in Metro Vancouver likely means fresh snow falling on the snowshoe trails in the mountains. In addition, pay attention to the season (too early or too late and the snow may be patchy), as snowshoeing over dirt is no fun! Also remember that fresh snow is easier, softer and much quieter to walk on than hard-packed snow with ice in it. Plan for safety just as you would with hiking. Follow the Safety & Security Planning section in this book, along with the ten activity safety essentials to prepare properly for your snowshoe. Good-quality, properly fit and well-broken-in hiking boots are a good investment. Have a plan for your snowshoe and know your limits and the limits of those adventuring with you.

This chapter covers two snowshoeing trips on Mount Seymour and two that begin on Cypress Mountain. The Go Further activity leads you to Squamish for the fifth and final activity. Reviewing your favourite hikes and doing a little research to ensure they are not in avalanche zones, or are too difficult to reach in the winter, may be useful. There are many other great snowshoe trails in southwestern British Columbia but few snowshoe guidebooks. The following notes apply to *all* snowshoe activities in this chapter. Enjoy the winter!

Dogs: At Cypress Mountain, Mount Seymour and Elfin Lakes have your dog on-leash while on park trails. These are all BC Park areas and there are fines if your dog is caught off-leash.

Transit/Bus: There is no public transit service to any of the snowshoe activities listed in this chapter. However, there are mountain shuttles:

- *Shuttle Bus – Mount Seymour:* The shuttle runs from Lonsdale Quay and from the base of Mount Seymour via the Parkgate Community Centre to the parking area at Mount Seymour. The cost is approximately $10 each way. The shuttle schedule can be found at mountseymour.com.

- *Shuttle Bus – Cypress Mountain:* Cypress Coach Lines leaves from Park Royal Shopping Centre (and also from Richmond Centre, Kitsilano, the West End and Lonsdale Quay). The cost is approximately $25 return, but better deals apply if you hold a U-pass or have a student card. The shuttle schedule is at cypressmountain.com.

Trail Reports: These are available online at BC Parks (env.gov.bc.ca/bcparks). Look under the headings for Cypress, Seymour and Garibaldi provincial parks. Be familiar with the reports prior to your snowshoe.

Snowshoe Rentals: Retailers such as Mountain Equipment Co-op (mec.ca) in Vancouver or North Vancouver or Deep Cove Outdoors (deepcoveoutdoors.com) will save you money over renting on either mountain.

Seasonal Snow Levels: Ensure there are sufficient snow levels. Do this by going to the Cypress Mountain and Mount Seymour websites to look at the snow base. Typically, you should be fine anytime between Christmas and early May.

Parking: Parking at Mount Seymour Provincial Park and Cypress Mountain is free. However, it is very busy on winter weekends and it's often difficult to find parking if you don't arrive early enough.

Safety: Have you read the Safety & Security Planning section of this book yet? If not, be aware that it is possible to get lost in our local mountains, so come prepared.

Winter Gear: Winter gear to carry is different from summer gear. Consider adding warm drinks, toques, gloves, extra layers, headlamps and sunglasses for snow shine. Shoe treads are handy if it's icy and bum pads are useful for a quick bum slide down some slopes (if you remembered to bring water-resistant pants).

Backcountry Permits: A free backcountry access day pass is required for snowshoeing on Cypress Mountain. This is necessary even if the trails are in the provincial park area, since you need to cross the resort grounds for BC Park backcountry access. The passes are free and you get them at Cypress Mountain Guest Services.

Paid Trails: Both Mount Seymour and Cypress Mountain also offer groomed trails that you pay to use. Maps are available at both mountains for these trails.

Family fun during a first snowfall of the season

Mount Seymour's Dog Mountain Trail & Overlook

Distance: 6 km
Time: 1.5 – 2 hrs.
Level: moderate
Grade: moderate < 75 m

Activity Highlight

The Dog Mountain Lookout is, without a doubt, my favourite place to be on a clear winter day. The view is outstanding! The distance, terrain and diversity of this snowshoe are as close to being "just right" as any trail can offer. The best days are the ones that are crystal-clear but follow a snowfall providing you with a soft, quiet walk among the

Snowshoeing in the low light of the afternoon as it filters through the trees is a magical experience. (PHOTO COURTESY OF LEE HALLIDAY PHOTOGRAPHY)

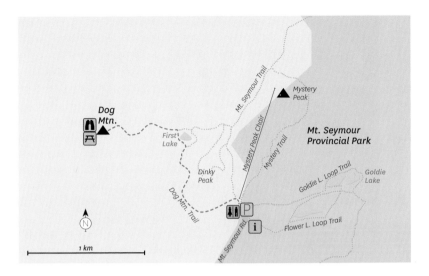

old-growth, subalpine forest. No new snow means loud crunching, making it harder to hear your companions. Be alert this winter for the perfect day!

Directions

Start at the Mount Seymour Trail kiosk, to the left of the Mystery Peak chairlift. Travel 50 metres up the main Mount Seymour trail and make your first left where you will go over a small bridge. This is the start of the mostly undulating Dog Mountain trail. On the weekends, there will often be people at this trailhead (and throughout the trail). The trail to First Lake (2.2-km return) has small challenges to help you learn how to walk on snowshoes effectively. Once you can master that, continue a further 2 km past the lake to reach Dog Mountain summit (6-km return from the parking area). Another option on this activity is to go east at First Lake (to your right if you are going toward Dog Mountain and left if you are returning), climb a 15-minute hill and return via the main Mount Seymour trail, thereby making this a partial loop.

TOP: *The winter world is just as amazing at the micro level. Watch for hoar frost on winter days.* (PHOTO COURTESY OF ROB ALEXANDER)

BOTTOM: *Grey jays spreading joy and to see what you might have for them*

Notes

Maps: These are available online at env.gov.bc.ca/bcparks. Look under Mount Seymour Provincial Park.

Restrooms: These are found in the Mount Seymour parking area only.

Safety: Have you read the Safety & Security Planning section of this book yet? If not, be aware that it's possible to get lost in the mountains, so come prepared.

Company: This is a highlight snowshoe in Metro Vancouver on a clear day. It is suitable for most people who are reasonably active. Share this trail with someone who is interested in, but has little experience on, snowshoes. The average teenager will be duly impressed, but you may not know it when they are with you, only when you hear them ask you for advice when they want to impress a date later!

Of Interest: This is an amazing snowshoe to do on a clear night with a full, or nearly complete, moon. Bring a headlamp, too, as this is truly one of the special winter adventures in Metro Vancouver.

See what you can pick out from the viewpoint, such as Lions Gate Bridge, Vancouver Island, Point Roberts, Stanley Park, Burns Bog, the University of British Columbia or Simon Fraser University. Notice Vancouver's early grid-lined streets.

Look for the North Shore Rescue cabin when at First Lake.

Eco-Insight: Subalpine Winter Survival

Mount Seymour is a superb location to plan a winter overnight trip and build a snow shelter. However, I would never suggest you attempt it without proper knowledge of the mountains and the ten activity safety essentials (see page 30) to keep you warm, dry, hydrated and capable of caring for yourself and others in the event of an emergency. So now consider the wildlife living at high altitudes and what they must do to survive. Alpine species need to adjust to colder temperatures, shorter growing seasons, more ultraviolet light, less water, poorer soil, more wind and longer lasting or permanent frost. They survive through adaptation. Just as we adapt with air conditioners in

Phoenix and heaters in Inuvik, or wear Gore-Tex for rain and wool for warmth, mountain species adapt too.

For example, the crow-sized bird called Clark's nutcracker collects seeds in the summer months and stores them throughout the mountains for winter food. They can collect and store as many as 100,000 seeds in summer and relocate up to 70 per cent of them during the winter. The slightly-larger-than-a-mouse-sized pika gathers dried grass in the summer to make minihaystacks throughout its territory. After the first insulating snow layer falls, the pika creates tunnels between the haystacks for its winter nutrition. Marmots simply sleep deeply for more than half the year. Hibernation sharply reduces metabolic levels, lengthening the time they are able to live off fat stored from summer feeding. During hibernation, their breathing is slow (only two breaths per minute), their heart rate drops (five beats per minute), their body temperature drops (from 37°C to only a few degrees above freezing!) and they are likely to cuddle up in groups to conserve body heat.

Other Area Interests

If you plan to extend your day in this area, I have two suggestions: Deep Cove for lunch, doughnuts or hot drinks; and the Lower Seymour Conservation Reserve (LSCR) for an easy walk to, and around, Rice Lake. The former will take you to a lookout of Indian Arm from Panorama Park. The latter will take you past the Seymour Water Filtration Plant and twin tunnels that connect the plant to the Capilano Reservoir. The twin tunnels are 3.8 metres in diameter, 7.1 kilometres long and 160 – 640 metres below ground – going under Grouse Mountain!

Mount Seymour's Dinky Peak City View Loop

Distance: 2.1 km
Time: 30 min. – 1.5 hrs.
Level: easy
Grade: easy < 50 m

Activity Highlight

This is among the shortest, quickest ways to get to a view over Vancouver while on snowshoes. It really belongs in the picnic section of this book, as the effort to reach it is minimal. So if you are looking for a quick snowshoe, then add this loop to your recreational repertoire.

Directions

This is a good spot to entice "newbies" to the sport. At the far end of the parking area is the Mount Seymour Trail kiosk. Begin here and walk uphill on the main Mount Seymour trail (the ski run is to your right). After about 15 minutes, a junction will be on your left. Turn left onto this and left again after 25 metres onto a small trail through the trees. Follow this for about 15 minutes to Dinky Peak. The trail is relatively easy to follow through the forested terrain and after ten minutes it leads up to the summit area where there are good views of Metro Vancouver. From the peak, watch for a trail to complete this as a loop that will take you back to the main Mount Seymour trail. If you want a longer snowshoe, return the same way to the junction near the main mountain trail. Turn left and drop down for ten minutes to First Lake then go left again to circle back to the parking area (it's about 20 minutes to the lake and another 20 minutes to the parking lot from the top of Dinky Peak).

Notes

Maps: These are available online at env.gov.bc.ca/bcparks. Search for Mount Seymour Provincial Park.

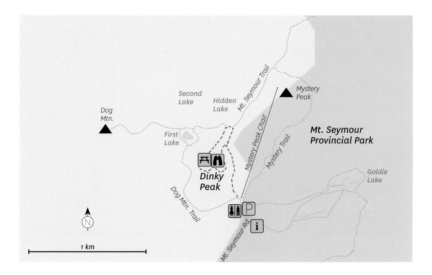

Restrooms: These are available in the Mount Seymour parking area only.

Safety: Have you read the Safety & Security Planning section of this book yet? If not, be aware that it's possible to get lost in the mountains, so come prepared.

Company: This is a superb date night snowshoe (but don't forget the spiked hot chocolate!) or an introductory snowshoe to get someone new to this sport interested. Moreover, if you have Christmas visitors, consider this snowshoe if they are fit and active.

Of Interest: Similar to Dog Mountain, this is also a great full-moon snowshoe, where you can pack your hot chocolate and bum pads to sit and enjoy the view of the city.

When my boys were young, I used this as an easy winter camping destination. The heavy overnight backpacks were easier to carry the short distance, and the payoff of the view was superb. We built a snow cave to sleep in for the night, but you can also bring a sturdy tent. Consider children if you are planning this activity.

Snowshoes vary in shapes and size. Be sure to get something for your weight and that can be put on or taken off with ease. Poles are an important addition for stability. (PHOTO COURTESY OF LEE HALLIDAY PHOTOGRAPHY)

Because we all like to play! Snowshoeing is great for all ages.

Eco-Insight: Alpine Species Adaptations

To adapt to harsh conditions, alpine birds grow thicker plumages, marmots hibernate, hummingbirds migrate and snowshoe hares have large feet. What have you done lately to adapt to harsh alpine conditions? Chances are your answer may include the purchase of a down jacket, sturdy boots with thick socks, a four-season tent or a winter sleeping bag. The fact is plants and animals adapt in many, many ways. These adaptations allow plants to play a specific role, that is, to find a specific niche, in their environment. Ptarmigan change their colour to blend into their surroundings, while a mountain goat's stomach has multiple chambers that result in internal heat generation during digestion. Frogs have glycerol in their bodies, allowing them to freeze solid without dying. Pikas don't hibernate; instead, they have adapted to high alpine conditions. For example, pikas have large, Mickey Mouse-style ears, helping them hear unseen predators above the snow in winter while also improving their ability to shed heat in summer.

In the alpine, the trees are shorter, their branches are tighter to the trunk and their needles are stiffer, allowing them to survive heavy snow. Plants below the snow use the energy they gathered from last summer's sunlight, stored in their roots, as they prepare to send flowers up at snowmelt. Other plants grow their roots and rhizomes deep underground and wait years to send their first leaves above the surface, ensuring they are well established before venturing into the harsh environment above. Some plants have natural antifreeze, while others have stems akin to fibre optics, allowing the sun to penetrate to their soil-bound roots. Some plants insulate with hair, while others grow thick, succulent leaves to store water. Some trees are insulated from fire with thick bark, while others create cones that actually require the heat of fire to open them. Ultimately, the adaptations are as varied as the species themselves. So, again, what have you done to adapt?

Other Area Interests

Do you know a bufflehead from a Barrow's goldeneye? For an extension to your day, take the Dollarton Highway in North Vancouver to Cates Park or Maplewood Flats for an additional walk near the water. There you are likely to see some birds that overwinter in Metro Vancouver, including goldeneyes and buffleheads – don't forget to bring your binoculars and bird book.

Cypress Mountain's Bowen Lookout over Howe Sound

Distance: 3 km
Time: 1 – 2 hrs.
Level: moderate
Grade: moderate < 100 m

Activity Highlight

Do you know someone you would like to entice to snowshoe for the first time? The Bowen Lookout trail may be the right activity on a clear day. You can rent snowshoes at the ski base, find the trail easily and, with a little uphill push, you will end up at a panoramic view of Howe Sound, the Sunshine Coast and Vancouver Island. Pack a thermos with hot tea and some homemade baking and you may get them hooked on the sport.

Looking west over Howe Sound and its islands
(PHOTO COURTESY OF VALERIE BELANGER)

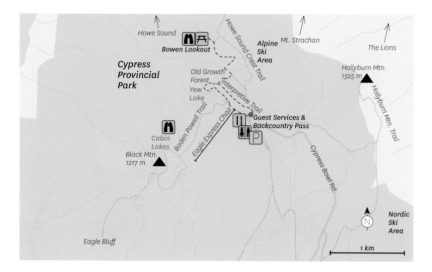

Directions

Obtain a free backcountry pass at guest services near the downhill ski area. Continue past the lodge and past the employees posted at the winter fence separating the downhill ski area from the lodge. Continue 100 metres past the Eagle Express chairlift and along the left side of the ski run coming off Mount Strachan (to your right). Turn left 90 degrees at the signpost for Bowen Lookout. Continue for ten minutes, and then turn right (away from Yew Lake). Follow the trail across the flat meadow for ten minutes. The trail will enter an old-growth forest on the far side of the meadow. There is an interesting five-minute interpretive loop trail in the old growth, which is well worth visiting. Continue through the old-growth forest for five minutes, and then turn left on the broad logging road heading west. Follow the road for 500 metres and cross a small bridge to the right across a small creek. The bridge may be covered with snow in winter. Zigzag up the steep trail for 20 minutes. Watch for a trail to the left. A five-minute snowshoe on this will take you to the Bowen Lookout. If you want to do a round trip, return from Bowen Lookout to the first junction, turn left and continue up the hill for ten minutes. You will reach the Howe Sound Crest trail and a signboard. Turn right and after ten minutes you will reach a flat bench road. This will lead you back to the ski area.

Snowshoes have evolved to a simple strapping system to make them easy to put on and remove. (PHOTO COURTESY OF LEE HALLIDAY PHOTOGRAPHY)

The Bowen Lookout trail is part of the 30-km Howe Sound Crest Trail that follows the mountain ridges north to Porteau Cove. There is a Howe Sound Crest trail brochure available online at env.gov.bc.ca/bcparks.

Notes

Maps: These are available online at env.gov.bc.ca/bcparks under the heading for Cypress Provincial Park.

Restrooms: These are available in the Cypress Mountain parking area only.

Safety: Have you read the Safety & Security Planning section of this book yet? If not, be aware that it's possible to get lost in the mountains, so come prepared.

Company: This activity is good for kids or people who don't have a lot of snowshoeing experience. Note there is a hill climb of about 90 metres of switchbacks – a good challenge for children.

Of Interest: This short snowshoe provides a rewarding view of Howe Sound, Bowen Island and the Sunshine Coast. A longer, steeper trail branches off to the left at the trailhead to Black Mountain and onward to Eagle Bluffs – a popular snowshoe trail as well.

As this is a relatively short activity, you can add extra time on the Howe Sound Crest Trail (HSCT). If this interests you, pick up the North Shore Trail Map 1:20,000 at Mountain Equipment Co-op and follow the HSCT north just before you reach the lookout.

Eco-Insight: Howe Sound & Glaciation

Howe Sound is a fjord – a valley deeply eroded by a glacier many millennia ago, now flooded by seawater. On a global scale, the fjord-rich coastline of British Columbia is truly grand. Viewed from the Bowen Lookout, Howe Sound's steep angled walls are readily apparent. These walls funnel air southward down Howe Sound, resulting in the "Squamish Wind." This wind is associated with winter arctic outflows, but it also provides strong breezes year-round. Kitesurfers make great use of this at the Squamish training dyke, but kayakers in the inlet should know to be careful as this strong wind can rise with little notice, changing a beautiful day trip into an emergency. The same steep walls have created some of the province's greatest traffic hazards as well. Debris flows from above have been known to carry mud, logs, gravel and boulders the size of cars onto the Sea-to-Sky Highway. Although it's not uncommon to have the highway closed for hours due to debris falling down the valley walls, provincial highway engineers are always working to design slide-mitigation structures.

At the head of this inlet lie Squamish and its namesake river. The milky green of the water is due to suspended glacial sediment transported from the Coast Mountains, and as far away as the Pemberton Icefield. Look west to see Bowen Island, and a small island nearby called Keats. Look northwest for Gambier and Anvil islands. Many children went to summer camp on one of these islands – did you?

Icicles on mountain hemlock (PHOTO COURTESY OF LEE HALLIDAY PHOTOGRAPHY)

Other Area Interests

Extend your day with a visit to the West Vancouver Seawall. In fact, on a sun-filled spring day, this is what Metro Vancouver is famous for – a morning snowshoe in the mountains, hot drinks in Dundarave Village at lunch and a mid-afternoon walk on the West Vancouver Seawall.

Cypress Mountain's Hollyburn Peak & Lions View

Distance: 7 km
Time: 3 – 4 hrs.
Level: difficult (see Notes)
Grade: difficult < 450 m

Activity Highlight

There is no getting around it, this snowshoe is a challenge. This is one of the more difficult of the popular snowshoeing trails on the North Shore due to its consistent climb and an especially steep section in the last quarter of the trail. The trail requires good technique. You must use the crampons on your snowshoes when you are coming back downhill on the slick, steep sections. I highly recommend poles to ease your way down the steep parts of the trail near the top.

Difficulty aside, the payoff of this snowshoe on a clear day is a view of the popular Vancouver peaks called the Lions. At the high point, it will feel as though you can reach out and touch them. The view is only one reason this snowshoe climb feels so good; the other is the feeling you have climbed your own little Mount Everest!

Directions

Park at the cross-country ski area and look for the trail between the ticket area and the main road. The trail goes north and uphill just behind the ticketing booth.

Notes

Maps: These are available online at env.gov.bc.ca/bcparks under the heading for Cypress Provincial Park.

Restrooms: These are available in the Cypress Mountain parking area only.

Safety: Have you read the Safety & Security Planning section of this

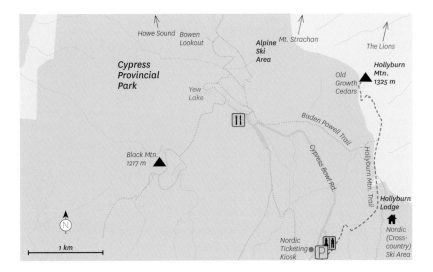

Great view of the Lions from Hollyburn Peak

(PHOTO COURTESY OF ROB ALEXANDER)

book yet? If not, be aware that it's possible to get lost in the mountains, so come prepared.

Of Interest: My recommendation is to tackle this challenge only after you are quite comfortable on snowshoes and when the day is clear. I'd also suggest bringing something on which to "butt-slide," such as old nylon pants or a plastic pad. There are a number of spots on your return that you can slide to descend fast, easily and safely.

Eco-Insight: Subalpine Old-Growth Forests

Consider the short growing season of the trees atop Hollyburn Peak. Growth begins after the snow melts, when frost disappears and when overnight temperatures creep above freezing. It's only then that sap begins to flow. So when you're at the top, find a tree to put your arms around and gauge its diameter. It grows for only a few months (approximately May – October), and as it does it grows slowly. What do you think its annual growth rings look like? Chances are they are very close together, possibly so close a magnifier would be required to see the separations between the rings! If you compare these subalpine trees to trees of similar diameter at lower elevations, such as those in Stanley Park, the subalpine trees will be far older. Here trees as thick as your lower leg could be considered old-growth (more than 250 years), but they are still small due to the harsh subalpine environment. Well known for its 1,000-year-old yellow cedars, this area also holds long-standing mountain hemlocks and subalpine firs.

Trees in these harshest of subalpine areas group together for protection from the elements. Groups of trees, called krummholz, in turn offer great microclimates where other species can take shelter. Leaning away from the prevailing wind, these groups of trees have low-lying branches called tree skirts that keep the ground temperature around their roots warmer than the air above. The trees themselves offer a windbreak and help create a milder environment on their leeward side for other plants or trees to establish themselves.

Have you heard of the BC Big Tree Registry (see bcbigtree.ca, which has great search features for different regions)? If you are in North Vancouver, you can search by region and find details on the largest trees in the area.

Snowshoeing is a great way to get a group of friends together.

(PHOTO COURTESY OF LEE HALLIDAY PHOTOGRAPHY)

Other Area Interests

If you happen to do this snowshoe on a Saturday afternoon in the winter, ask about what may be happening at the rustic Hollyburn Lodge for the evening. Locals often snowshoe or ski one kilometre into the lodge on Saturdays for live music or a meal at the small food kiosk inside. More information on these music evenings can be found at cypressmountain.com/hollyburn-music.

Go Further: Paul Ridge toward Diamond Head & Elfin Lakes – Squamish

Distance: 14 km
Time: 4 – 6 hrs.
Level: difficult
Grade: difficult < 625 m

Activity Highlight

One could say this snowshoe is well beyond the level of the other snowshoeing activities in this chapter. The distance is much greater, the elevation is greater and the backcountry nature of it will feel more remote. However, it is my intention to lead you further, both geographically and physically, and the reality of this snowshoe is it's a consistent, but moderate, uphill snowshoe on an old road. It's never too steep, and as long as you prepare for a long day (such as bringing plenty of water and food), then this is a very doable activity for those who wish to challenge themselves to "go further" physically. In good weather, the payoff is its incredible beauty and how different it can feel compared to snowshoeing on the North Shore Mountains.

Directions

Take Highway 99 (Sea-to-Sky) north from Metro Vancouver and continue 3.75 km past the turnoff to downtown Squamish. Turn right on Mamquam Road off Highway 99 and continue 14 km on this secondary road. At the main fork in the road, veer left and continue to the Diamond Head parking area (or to the area that is plowed). Contact the Squamish Adventure Centre (tourismsquamish.com) to inquire about road conditions. Please note that this road is secondary and although my Honda Civic with snow tires and chains has made it, I'd recommend a 4x4. Plan approximately two hours from downtown Vancouver to drive to the Diamond Head parking area.

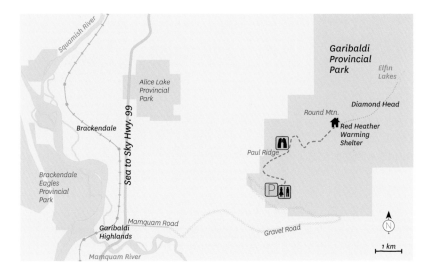

Notes

Maps: These are available online at env.gov.bc.ca/bcparks under the heading for Garibaldi Provincial Park.

Views on the way to Elfin Lakes (PHOTO COURTESY OF JACQUELINE SLAGLE)

Restrooms: These are available at the warming hut, at the summit (outhouses) and at the parking area. Bring your own toilet paper.

Safety: Have you read the Safety & Security Planning section of this book yet? If not, be aware that it's possible to get lost in the mountains, so come prepared.

Of Interest: This is part of Garibaldi Provincial Park, a park that is among the most loved jewels on the south coast for its geology, natural beauty, wildlife and proximity to Vancouver. This means it is busy all year long. Expect many people in the area, especially on sunny weekends.

The trail is steeper (a moderate, but consistent, hill) until about 4.5 km, where you reach the Red Heather Shelter. Another 2.5 km to Paul Ridge takes you to the high point.

For those who want to continue their snowshoe in the alpine, the trail continues 4 km more to Elfin Lakes and another shelter. If you add this, it will make your total trip 22 km – a full day!

Eco-Insight: Snow Science

While climbing the trail to Paul Ridge, contemplate the importance of snow. Snow provides habitat for a diversity of creatures, both on its surface, including birds and large mammals, and underneath, where a variety of small mammals and plants take advantage of its super-insulating qualities. The upper surface of snow is the same as the air temperature, sometimes very cold, but close to the ground it's closer to 0°C. If you're a pika, it's a relatively warm place to be.

Entire ecosystems exist within a snowpack. These ecosystems begin with cryophiles – creatures that can survive at, or below, the freezing point. Watch for pink colouration on large snow patches. This cryophile is red algae, otherwise known as watermelon snow. Feeding on the algae are bacteria, fungi, snow worms and snow fleas; higher up on the food chain are mites, spiders, finches, wrens and, ultimately, top predators such as golden eagles.

You can also think of the snowpack as a water reservoir, similar to how a dam stores water in a lake. Steady warming over the spring and summer provides the invaluable service of a gradual release of water

Watch for mountain goats on the Paul Ridge snowshoe.

(PHOTO COURTESY OF CAM ANDERSON)

throughout the seasons – and it's free! In addition to annual snow accumulation, glaciers provide a supplementary freshwater supply that helps preserve natural flows to our regions' rivers, which are used in BC to irrigate crops and to produce hydroelectricity. A warming planet with shrinking glaciers and a smaller snowpack is having far-reaching effects on our environment. Water flow, habitat and entire ecosystems (even those yet to be discovered) are being diminished and possibly lost altogether. While enjoying your hike, think of the snow under your feet as a security blanket that supports our natural ecosystems and our ability to provide our communities with food and energy.

Other Area Interests

If you are a new visitor to Squamish, then be sure to take a stroll in the estuary for a great view of the Stawamus Chief (the "Chief" is a summer hike worth coming back to Squamish for). For more information on this hike, see the Stawamus Chief hike on page 104 in the hiking chapter of this book.

Cycling

"Life is like riding a bicycle. To keep your balance you must keep moving."
—Albert Einstein, Letter to His Son Eduard, February 5, 1930

Metro Vancouver is a cycling mecca. Whether people are demanding transportation alternatives to the automobile, or whether local government is taking a "build it and they will come" approach, the important point is there are more safe cycling opportunities today than ever in Vancouver's history. Examples of new cycling infrastructure include roads with separated bicycle lanes, increased bicycle parking, an increasing set of roads dedicated to cycling that crisscross the city and the option of putting your bike on a transit bus, the West Coast Express or the SkyTrain. Cycling in Metro Vancouver is simply an easier option to choose than ever before and it's all because of the region's strong support for green transportation initiatives, which make roads safer and more comfortable for cycling. In 2015 the City of Vancouver plans to launch a public bike share system (PBS), making bicycles available for short-term use by the public for a fee.

This chapter explores nine unique cycling activities that range from the urban city core, to the outlying suburbs and even one trip through rural southern Vancouver Island. The following adventures utilize dyke systems, seawalls, forest trails, gravel paths, paved pathways and quiet side roads where possible. The routes take you deep into a watershed, among old-growth forests, along serene river edges, beside the ocean and up to clifftop overlooks. They direct you through a local fishing village, around wine orchards and farming fields and among city street art installations. Finally, the trips will lead you to the heart of the city, to the suburbs, to the Fraser Valley and on to such destinations as Vancouver Island and Point Roberts in Washington state.

If you have not been on a bike for a while, don't forget that when on a road, cyclists have the same rights and responsibilities as drivers. But your thinking should especially focus on your responsibilities – you are softer and more breakable than a car! BC's Motor Vehicle Act applies to bicycles, too, and that means coming to a full rest at stop signs, using front and rear lights on your bicycle after dark, signalling before turning, wearing an approved helmet and not riding on sidewalks unless posted signs allow it.

There are additional safety tips to consider when cycling.

- Never assume other cyclists, drivers or pedestrians see you. Making eye contact with other road users is essential.

- Learn to share the road and be predictable in your behaviour.

- Take extra care when cycling past parked cars, always leaving space for a car door to be opened.

- Yield to pedestrians crossing the street, and to buses when they are leaving a stop.

Just past 9 km on the Seymour Pathway there is an opportunity to visit an old-growth forest. I recommend getting off your bikes to walk through this special ecosystem. Know a teen who you would enjoy spending time with? This is a great ride for teenagers.

(PHOTO COURTESY OF CHRISTINE GAIO)

- Maintain your bike in good working order and equip it with front and rear lights and a warning bell.

- Don't wear headphones or use electronic devices while riding.

- Take extra caution when roads are wet.

Whether one of these activities gets you back on your bike again, becomes a new route in your existing cycling repertoire or provides a reason to learn cycling for the first time, you can be certain each of these activities will inspire you. Cycling for leisure or transportation can be convenient and comfortable, fashionable and fun. Ultimately, cycling improves our health, environment and the communities we live in. Before you know it, you may be biking to school, to work, on local errands, with transit and with friends and family. If this becomes the beginning of further cycling in your life, then consider the following resources specific to cycling in Metro Vancouver:

- *Bike Sense*, put out by the Greater Victoria Cycling Coalition, is a comprehensive BC guide, written and reviewed by professional cycling skills instructors, that details how to operate a bike in traffic;

- Cycle Vancouver (cyclevancouver.ubc.ca) is a website that offers an interactive route planner (it suggests the best cycling route between destinations);

- TransLink (translink.ca/en/Getting-Around/Cycling) has cycling route maps, as does the bicycle-mapping feature in Google Maps (google.ca/maps).

Boundary Bay Dyke Bike

Distance: 40 km
Time: 2.5 – 3 hrs.
Level: moderate
Grade: easy < 5 m
Public Transit Routes: 603, 604, C84
Surface: gravel

Activity Highlight

Picture this. A south-wind sea breeze blows while riding on a pancake-flat dyke with wetlands on one side and working farms on the other – this is quintessential Boundary Bay. From just about anywhere on the dyke, look north on a clear spring day and turn your head slowly clockwise to take in snow-capped peaks from the North Shore ski hills to Golden Ears. Keep turning, to the North Cascades…turn a little more, to Mount Baker, and finally turn due south toward the San

There are many kilometres of dyke to cycle along Boundary Bay.
(PHOTO COURTESY OF CHRISTINE GAIO)

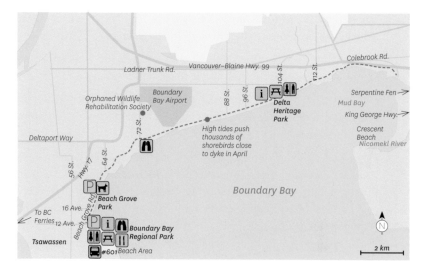

Juan Islands (Orcas Island looks like a giant turtle) and Point Roberts. How is that for a view? Begin your ride at Beach Grove Park and go east until, well, until you're half-tired. Then go west to complete!

Directions

As you ride east on the dyke, you pass 64th, 72nd, 88th, 96th, 104th and 112th (12.5 km one-way) streets. You can keep riding into Surrey to Railway Avenue (another 5.5 km one-way). A final extension would be to go north on Railway to Colebrook Road, turn east, continue to King George Highway and then south on a side trail to Serpentine Fen.

Notes

Maps: These can be accessed online at metrovancouver.org/services/parks_lscr/regionalparks or free at Metro Vancouver Parks. Search for the Boundary Bay Regional Park map.

Restrooms: These are available at Boundary Bay Regional Park and at Railway Avenue in Surrey. There may be other porta-potties set up along the dyke, but don't count on it.

Safety: Don't forget to take into account the wind that comes off the bay, and the gravel trail, when planning this trip. These factor into the time it takes to complete the ride and increase fatigue.

Timing: This cycle can be done all year, though the winter to early spring provides opportunities to see many hawks and eagles.

Company: The flat dyke with great views makes this a fantastic spot for older adults, especially if they also happen to be birders. If you know one, ask them to join you.

Dogs: Rover should be on a leash while on the dyke, but Beach Grove Park, at the start of this ride, has an off-leash area. Boundary Bay is an internationally significant site on the Pacific Flyway migration route (see the Eco-Insight below), with hundreds of bird species using the area at different times of the year. Remember, dogs can stress wildlife immensely in species-rich areas like this. Please keep your dog on a leash and keep to the main dyke.

Of Interest: High tides give you opportunities to see more wildlife close up while on your ride, while low tides give you an opportunity to walk far out on the ocean's sandy bottom at Beach Grove Park.

Eco-Insight: Sandpipers & Bacterial Slime

Boundary Bay, a stopover on the Pacific Flyway, is one of the richest and most important ecosystems for migrating and wintering birds in Canada. This is an internationally designated "Important Bird Area," one of thousands of globally recognized sites of particular significance to bird migration. Incredibly, as many as two million western sandpipers land in this region during their northward migration in late April. In fact, one-quarter of the global population of western sandpipers may be in this area on a single day! Sandpipers and other shorebirds travel from South and Central America, stopping over in San Francisco Bay, CA, Grays Harbor, WA, Fraser River Delta, BC, Stikine

OPPOSITE: *A winter trip to Boundary Bay can mean some good views of birds, including the snowy owl.* (PHOTO COURTESY OF CHRISTINE GAIO)
ABOVE: *When the tide is out, it is really out. It seems like you can walk forever out on the sand flats from Boundary Bay Regional Park.*
(PHOTO COURTESY OF LORI GEOSITS)

River Delta, BC, and finally completing their voyages in coastal Alaska. These species of birds have been making this journey for thousands of years and their migration route is so genetically inherent that even though the parents fly south as soon as four weeks after hatching their young, the juvenile birds, flying solo, know exactly where to fly later in the summer. The journey is thousands of miles long and the young birds are precise as they touch down to feed. At the weight of about three toonies each, these juvenile sandpipers know the specific locations for their migration – without ever having been there!

What makes Boundary Bay such a great place for them to stop? It's the biofilm: a thin, dense layer of microbes, organic waste and sediment all stuck to the mudflats in a mucous-like matrix. It's essentially, umm, snot that binds the micro-organisms to the mud, allowing the sandpipers to feast.

Unfortunately, there is intense pressure on this area for residential, recreational, airport, industrial and seaport expansion, as well as a great risk of pollution from residential and industrial development. Be in awe and tread lightly.

Other Area Interests

An extension to your day could include a visit to the Orphaned Wildlife Rehabilitation Society (OWL) on 72nd Street, where OWL rescues birds and other wildlife. OWL also has public displays.

Lower Seymour Conservation Reserve Pathway to Old-Growth Forest & Hatchery

Distance: 23 km
Time: 2 – 3 hrs.
Level: moderate
Grade: moderate < 50 m
Public Transit Route: 228 (see Notes)
Surface: paved/gravel

Activity Highlight

Here's a challenge for you. Name one other place in the world (just one) where you can cycle 22 km on a paved path, within a temperate forest and with no vehicles! I'll bet you can't. Now add old-growth forest to wander in as you stretch your legs, a rushing river to have your lunch beside, a fish hatchery to see local salmon close up and a dam holding back a vast water reservoir. If you were successful in locating another jewel such as this, would it be within 25 minutes of a city's downtown core? Come on – give up – this set of conditions must be unique. This paved pathway is exceptional and it makes for a great cycling day trip.

Directions

This is one of two *bike* activities outlined in this book in the Seymour Valley. The other is by mountain bike in the Other Adventures section. Take exit 22A off Highway 1 for Capilano University and continue 5 km north on Lillooet Road to the Rice Lake Gate parking area. In the reserve, follow the Seymour Valley Pathway to the 9-km mark. At the Stoney Creek picnic site, cross the road and continue downhill until you reach the Seymour River – a perfect picnic spot. Retrace your route 200 m and turn right to cycle and walk (highly recommended) in the old-growth forest for another 2 km to the Seymour Hatchery and Seymour Dam.

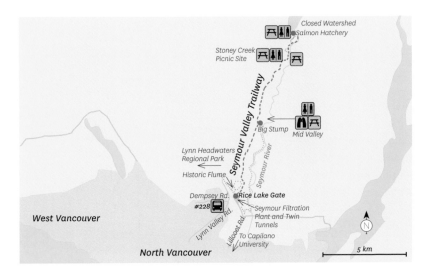

Notes

Transit & Transportation: Bus #228 goes to the edge of the Seymour Valley. From the corner of Dempsey and Lynn Valley Road, you will have to walk 500 m to the start at Rice Lake Gate.

Maps: These can be located at Metro Vancouver Parks or at the Rice Lake Gate. Ask for the Lower Seymour Conservation Reserve (LSCR) map.

Restrooms: These are located at the Rice Lake Gate and at various points on the Seymour Pathway.

Safety: Be aware you may be sharing the paved pathway with roller-bladers, walkers, other cyclists and runners. The rolling hills allow you to pick up speed that might create a hazardous situation if you are not careful.

Timing: April to October is the best time for this ride due to snow often settling in the upper valley during the winter months.

Company: This is a good family ride and, although it has many hills, it's a good challenge for active children.

Near mid-valley on the Seymour Pathway is a side trail to a stump among the largest you have seen. Yes, trees were once this big on the North Shore.

Dogs: Canine companions are not permitted north of the Rice Lake Gate.

Of Interest: There is a nice picnic spot on the Seymour River at the 10-km mark. Pack your picnic in your panniers and pick a spot on the river's edge. This spot should be a quiet, tranquil area, but, incredibly, you are only 20 km (as the crow flies) to downtown Vancouver. Please be sure to leave no trace that you were ever there. This is truly a special spot.

Please walk your bikes in the old-growth forest. Lock your bike to a tree and spend time walking the old-growth forest trails. This is more magical on foot. One suggestion is to choose a rain-soaked day to visit. This is when the old-growth forest is in its glory.

Eco-Insight: Watersheds

Do you know where your water comes from? If you live in Metro Vancouver, chances are it passes through the LSCR. The road you are riding on parallels a water pipe that moves water from the LSCR to Metro Vancouver. In fact, more than two-thirds of Metro Vancouver residents get their water from here or from the Capilano watershed, and all of it goes through the Seymour water filtration plant near the parking area. As you arrive, notice the twin tunnels that connect the filtration plant to the Capilano Reservoir. The twin tunnels are 3.8 m in diameter, 7.1 km in length and 160 – 640 m below ground – travelling a direct route under Grouse Mountain! The LSCR is not a park but rather the source of our domestic water supply and has supplied the invisible water pipes of Metro Vancouver for over a century. It is important for a city's residents to know the details of the infrastructures that surround and support us – both nature's and society's. To gauge your understanding, check out the Bioregional Quiz at the back of this book.

The crystal-clear water drains from the mountains that immediately surround Seymour Lake, through the old-growth conifer forest that drapes its sides. The water settles in the lake before it moves through pipes for chlorination, filtration and distribution into the water utility system. To protect the integrity of our water supply, the watershed above the dam remains closed to the public.

How much have you paid for bottled water? Our tap water is arguably some of the world's best drinking water, and according to Metro Vancouver, it costs only $0.0008 per litre! Would you like to know more about how much water and oil it takes to make one bottle of water? If so, look at Metro Vancouver's tap water page at metrovancouver. org/region/Pages/TapWater.aspx.

Other Area Interests

Capilano University campus is worth a walk around, though parking may be difficult to find on a weekday with its 7,500-plus student population. The Bosa Centre for Film and Animation is one highlight of this campus.

Point Roberts, WA, International Cycle Loop

Distance: 18 – 20 km
Time: 1 – 2.5 hrs.
Level: moderate
Grade: moderate < 200 m
Public Transit Routes: 601, 602, SkyTrain/Canada Line
Surface: road/dirt

Activity Highlight

54-40 or fight. Do you know what this indicates? If you said it's a very good Vancouver rock band, you're correct, but where did that band get its name? In the mid-1840s, this was a slogan used by a US presidential candidate to take British territory by force to the line of 54 degrees and 40 minutes (geography-speak). The highlight of this ride *is* the 49th Parallel! Challenge yourself to do a little digging and understand how this line came to create this geopolitical oddity known as Point Roberts. If you find this fascinating, then dig just a little further and discover how the "Pig War" extended the international border through the Gulf and San Juan islands. Tuck your research into your panniers and pull it out at Lighthouse Park (the one in Point Roberts), Lily Point or Bay View, and feed your inner history buff. The story may lead you to consider a further ride to San Juan Island to experience more of the story.

Directions

First, don't forget your passport to cross the border! Cross the border on your bike. Turn right on Mackenzie, right on Delano and left on Roosevelt to begin your loop of Point Roberts. As you begin, all the homes on your right are in Canada, the simple ditch behind them is the dividing line between the two countries! Continue counter-clockwise, making sure to stop at the end of Roosevelt to reflect on the 49th Parallel monument erected in 1861. The road now becomes Marine

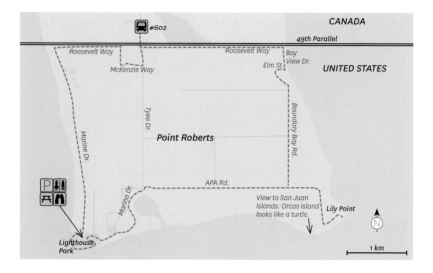

Drive. Make a detour to Lighthouse Park for a view of the Southern Gulf and San Juan Islands before continuing to APA Road (your first moderate hill). Turn right and ride to the Lily Point parking area. From here, decide on whether to take your bike with you or lock it to a tree. I suggest getting off your bike and hiking the trail to the point. Bring your pannier-packed picnic with you for a beach meal. If you take the trail that is due south out of the parking area, you'll arrive at the top of the bluffs for an amazing view. Follow these bluffs to a clear wide path that goes downhill to the beach (about 70 m below). Return to the top, follow APA Road to Boundary Bay Road and turn right. Follow this to Elm, turn right and then ride along the beach on Bay View. Finally, turn left on Roosevelt and return to the border. Note there are several signs telling you to turn off this road, as there is *no border access*. This road will come up on the north side of the border, but after asking at customs, I understand you can ride this road to the end at the border and then turn left to get to the US Customs before returning to Canada.

Notes

Maps: You can find maps of Point Roberts at local gas stations there. However, I'd suggest printing one off Google Maps prior to leaving.

View from the southern tip of Point Roberts at Lily Point looking east
(PHOTO COURTESY OF CHRISTINE GAIO)

Restrooms: These are at Lighthouse Park and Lily Point.

Dogs: Furry friends are not recommended due to road cycling and traffic.

Of Interest: There is beach access at the 49th Parallel monument if you walk down the trail in the forested area just south of the monument. The beach faces west toward Vancouver Island and the BC Ferries terminal.

Are you a stargazer but find the light in Metro Vancouver doesn't provide for a dark enough sky? Try Lighthouse Park in Point Roberts. It is one of the darker areas, with unobstructed views of the night sky.

Due to its geographic location, this is a great area to see ocean birds and eagles soaring alongside the cliffs.

Eco-Insight: Bigleaf Maples at Lily Point

As you walk the trail to Lily Point, notice the bigleaf maple trees that form the canopy overhead. Don't ever think that a tree is an island unto itself. This tree, which ranges from northern Vancouver Island to San Francisco, has much to offer its ecosystem.

- Bigleaf maples support the growth of great quantities of moss on their branches and trunks. The mosses then provide a substrate for licorice ferns and other plants to root in and grow off the trunks and branches of the bigleaf maples.

- Lichens hang off the branches, providing food for elk and deer when the ground is covered with snow. Scientists have calculated that the mosses and lichens contain up to four times greater mass than the bigleaf maple foliage itself!

- Mosses and lichens are also known as epiphytes because they extract their nutrients from the air, rain or debris that accumulates around them. Around the mosses and lichens, soil builds up in the canopy branches and the tree sends tiny roots out of its branches into the mossy soil to tap nutrients from the mosses (perhaps to collect rent!).

- Dinner-plate-sized leaves falling to the ground provide essential forms of potassium, calcium and nitrogen that help build and fertilize the soil as they decay. Many gardeners cover their gardens for winter with these leaves.

- The thick mossy branches supply nesting sites for many species of birds, offer homes for northern flying squirrels and provide "perches-with-views" for bald eagles.

- In the human realm, the trees are tapped for maple syrup, and their wood is used to make high-end furniture and flooring, the necks and backs of guitars and violins and that burl-wood table you play poker on at the cabin!

Other Area Interests

Vancouverites often see this area as a long way out of town, therefore you'll find less "recreational traffic" here. If you extend this day, some good choices are Centennial Beach Park in Boundary Bay, Fred Gingell Park in Tsawwassen or the Ladner Market if you happen to be there on the right summer weekend.

Traboulay PoCo Trail Loop

Distance: 25 km
Time: 1.5 – 2 hrs.
Level: easy
Grade: easy < 25 m
Public Transit Routes: 159, 160, C37, C38
Surface: gravel/paved

Activity Highlight

Suburbs often struggle with how to draw visitors to their area. The Traboulay PoCo Trail is a good reason to be a recreational tourist in Port Coquitlam (PoCo). It was visionary to connect the dots of dykes, parks and city green spaces to form a 25-km trail that now loops around the community. This cycling jewel encircling Port Coquitlam takes cyclists through a landscape that includes forests, creek and river areas, as well as marsh, meadows and urban landscapes while following the Pitt and Coquitlam rivers.

Cyclists can get stunning sunsets over the Fraser River from the PoCo trail.

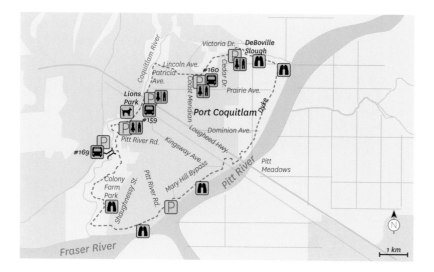

Directions

This trail is good to cycle in either direction and has many locations at which to start. Personally, I like to start at the Red Bridge (off Pitt River Road) and cycle clockwise toward Lions Park, Hyde Creek, DeBoville Slough and then return along the Pitt and Coquitlam rivers through Colony Farm. Due to the urban nature of this trail, the many user groups and the multiple crossroads, safe cycling is especially important, as is carrying a map with you (see Notes below).

Notes

Maps: These are located online at the Port Coquitlam Parks and Recreation website (portcoquitlam.ca/Recreation_and_Culture/Parks_ and_Trails).

Restrooms: These are located at many places along the trail.

Timing: If you are cycling this route in September and October, be sure to keep your eyes open for spawning salmon in the Coquitlam River.

Dogs: Furry pets should be on-leash while on the trails, but the 3300 Block of Shaughnessy Street has an off-leash park, as does the downtown area just off Gates Park at Maple Street and Bury Avenue.

A footbridge over the Coquitlam River on the PoCo trail

Of Interest: British Columbia has five species of salmon. Do you know what they are? All five call the Coquitlam River home. Read the Eco-Insight below after you try to name them. Also, consider the Bioregional Quiz at the end of this book in Appendix A.

The word "Coquitlam" comes from the Kwikwetlem First Nation, which means "red fish up the river," which is, in fact, what you will see if you cycle this trail in the fall!

Eco-Insight: Spawning Salmon

Salmon spawning in BC rivers, including the Coquitlam River along the PoCo trail, are truly one of the world's great natural wonders. The Coquitlam River is home to all five of BC's salmon species: pink, chum, coho, chinook and sockeye. In the fall, the migrating salmon reach their home rivers or creeks and pair up. When ready, a female locates pea-sized gravel and, using her tail, she sweeps away gravel to create a nest cavity (called a "redd") and releases her eggs. Her male partner will disperse sperm (called "milt") over the eggs as the female covers them with gravel. Both salmon soon die and decompose, providing nutrients from their bodies to the fertilized eggs in the area. By the following spring, the eggs mature to alevins, fry and, finally, smolts – think babies, children and teenagers. The smolts "smell" their home in

Sockeye salmon (PHOTO COURTESY OF LORI GEOSITS)

the river, commit the scent to memory and venture downriver to the ocean. Over the next several years in the ocean, they grow to become adults, collecting nutrients from far off in the Pacific and, in as few as four years, return to their home river to spawn in order to create a new generation. The salmon migrate upstream and are able to find their home river due to its unique smell, the scent they learned as smolts. This is their story in a nutshell, but consider the flow of nutrients and what this means to the greater ecosystem.

Nutrients from the open ocean help salmon grow into adults, and then salmon return to their home rivers and release these nutrients by way of their bodies to their young. In turn, these nutrients feed another entire ecosystem that you may not have guessed. To find out which ecosystem, read the Eco-Insight: Bears, Salmon & Temperate Forests (see page 188).

Other Area Interests

Port Coquitlam is the hometown of Terry Fox. If you've participated in the Terry Fox Run in your own community, then perhaps next fall you may wish to try the hometown run that leaves from Hyde Creek Recreation Centre. An extension to your day could include going to Leigh Square Community Arts Village or for some terrific gelato across from the Port Coquitlam courts.

Vancouver Biennale Art Ride

Distance: 15 – 60 km
Time: 1 – 4 hrs.
Level: moderate
Grade: moderate < 150 m
Public Transit Route: SkyTrain/Canada Line
Surface: pavement

Activity Highlight

London, Venice, Moscow, Vancouver, Kobe, New York and Sydney – what do all these world-class cities have in common? All these cities have a contemporary public art biennale installation. In Vancouver, the art is strategically located in many of the city's most attractive locations. Wouldn't you rather ditch your car and the hassles of finding parking around each art piece and instead hop on your bike and flow between the pieces on two wheels? An easy decision in this beautiful city; give it a try.

Directions

To do this cycle properly, you will need to go to the website vancouverbiennale.com and look at its suggested cycling routes. The biennale is a bi-annual public art exhibition that brings sculptures, new media and performance works from international artists and places the pieces around Metro Vancouver. The website offers a self-guided tour, called BIKEnnale, of the public art pieces it places around the city.

Notes

Maps: You can find maps of the art ride on the Vancouver Biennale website. This cycle will likely require a fair amount of riding on streets. However, Vancouver is increasingly getting more lanes and roads devoted to cyclists. Look on the City of Vancouver website (vancouver.ca/streets-transportation/cycling-routes-maps-and-trip-planner) or visit Mountain Equipment Co-op to obtain a city cycling map. The biennale map changes with this exhibit every two years.

Giving colour and fun to a cement plant at Granville Island

Restrooms: These will be available at various places along the route.

Safety: As some of this activity will be on city streets, know your safety skills and signs for cycling around vehicles if you have not done this for a while.

Timing: This is a great summer evening activity (but be sure to have proper reflective gear and lighting) and easily combined with a favourite downtown eatery as you move between the art installations in the downtown core.

Dogs: Canine companions are not appropriate for this cycling activity.

Of Interest: Guided, bicycle-led, art tours that explore Vancouver's vibrant collection of public art along the city's dedicated bike lanes are also possible. See vancouverbiennale.com for an inexpensive guided excursion.

A Vancouver Biennale sculpture that was so loved by the public, a crowdsourcing campaign was started to ensure it remained in this spot.
(PHOTO COURTESY OF LORI GEOSITS)

Eco-Insight: City-Dwelling Species

While touring the biennale route in Vancouver's urban landscape, consider the urban wildlife that share the area. Coyotes, raccoons and rats may get the most media attention, while deer, bears and cougars occasionally materialize. Pet owners often release rabbits, turtles and snakes into local green spaces, while urban trail walkers co-exist with squirrels, pigeons, starlings and house sparrows. What do all of these species have in common? In ecological terms, they're all considered generalists. That is, they are able to thrive in a wide variety of habitats and they survive on a diverse diet. As our environment changes, these species will likely adapt along with us.

On the one hand, urban wildlife offer plenty of opportunities for people to engage with species and have a very personal experience – a bird taking seed from your hand, a squirrel at your suet feeder or a raccoon leading her kits across your lawn. On the other hand, wild species are just that – wild – and encounters can be horrific: a coyote attacking a dog on a leash, a skunk nesting under your front steps or a bird dive-bombing your daughter to scare her away from a nest. Frequent contact with people generally makes wildlife bolder.

On this urban ride, watch for some city-dwelling species such as the coyote. (PHOTO COURTESY OF ROB ALEXANDER)

It is important to understand that food is a primary motivator for wildlife and to reconsider what you feed them, or even if you should feed them at all. Often we even feed wildlife unintentionally by leaving pet food outside or letting birdseed scatter to the ground, thereby attracting mice. If you do decide to feed wildlife, including the exhilaration of being able to share your lunch with a raven, jay or squirrel when you've reached a mountain peak, consider carrying sunflower seeds, unsalted nuts or millet to keep your effect to a minimum. But also consider the implications of doing even that, and maybe just talk to them instead.

Other Area Interests

The route will take you past Vancouver's most famous attractions, including Stanley Park, the West End, False Creek, Kitsilano and the University of British Columbia Endowment Lands. Extend your day where you please!

Richmond Bike Loop on Trails...or Mostly So

Distance: 33 km
Time: 2 – 3 hrs.
Level: moderate
Grade: easy < 25 m
Public Transit Routes: SkyTrain/Canada Line, 401, 402, 403
Surface: gravel/paved

Activity Highlight

What comes to mind when you think of Richmond? Here are some hints: 1) it's the delta of the Fraser River; 2) it's where Vancouver International Airport is located; 3) you can stand on the first floor of almost any building and see for miles! Yes, it's flat! This horizontal community makes it easier to cover more area in a shorter time and its highlight is the view over the Strait of Georgia as you cycle the dyke west from the Olympic Oval, past Terra Nova, to Steveston Village. However, plan time for en-route stops, as there are many reasons – especially in Steveston, for gelato or fish from the docks.

Directions

A good start to this loop around the city of Richmond is to begin with your bike on the Canada Line. The station you get on at will have an elevator to get your bike to the platform, and when you get off at Bridgeport Station, you can take the elevator to street level and begin your ride – "easy peasy"! Most of this ride is on a trail except for a small section near Bridgeport Station. Follow these directions to spend the "...or mostly so" time on trails and the least time on roads.

When you get to Bridgeport Station, go south on Great Canadian Way for one block on the side of the road. Go left (west) on Van Horne Way for 50 m to a cycling path on your right. Follow this under the Oak Street Bridge. The path leads to Shell Road. Ride the side of Shell Road past Bridgeport, Bird and Cambie to the underpass at Highway 99.

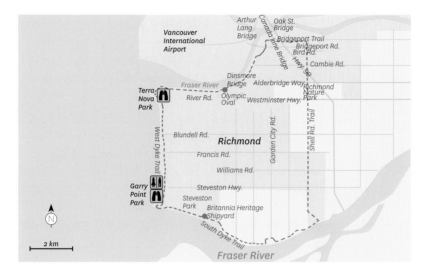

The Shell Road trail will now take you south to the Fraser River (total 10 km), west to Steveston Village and Garry Point via the dyke (total 20 km), then north to Terra Nova, east to the Richmond Oval (total 31 km) and back to the road section to Bridgeport Station (total 33.5 km). Note that the final section requires the road again. The shortest route on the road to Bridgeport Station takes you from the dyke to Cambie (go east), left on No. 3 Road northeast to Sea Island Way and then left on Garden City and north to the station.

Notes

Maps: You can find maps for cycling Richmond at the City of Richmond website (richmond.ca/services/ttp/cycling). I find maps are better when opened to a larger size than my printer can manage. Therefore, I suggest asking the City of Richmond to send one to you, which they will do free of charge.

Restrooms: These are located at various spots along the route, including Garry Point, Terra Nova and the Bridgeport area.

Safety: About 5 km of this activity will be on city streets. Know your safety skills and signs for riding on city streets if you have not cycled on roadways for a while.

Timing: Summer days are a delight on this trail, but weekdays are less busy than weekends.

Dogs: Your best friend should be on-leash while on the trail, but this is not suggested on roadways. The best section of this activity recommended for dogs is the Shell Road multi-use trail.

Of Interest: Richmond has taken an old railbed (think "rails to trails") and created the Shell Road multi-use trail – a corridor that dissects a good part of the city north to south to make this loop of the other three sides on the water possible. The idea of trail corridors through communities is becoming more common as we determine what makes a livable city. Look at the region you live in and identify where the connecting corridors are that could help your community move about off roads.

If you do take the Canada Line as suggested, an option is to get off at the Marine Drive Station on Cambie and cycle over the dedicated cycle path on the Canada Line Bridge (highly recommended if you are not afraid of heights).

Eco-Insight: Urban Trails

How important is it to have access to urban trails and natural landscapes near your home? Many urban dwellers put this among their top priorities when choosing a location in which to live. Access to urban parks, dyke systems, bike paths, seawalls and ravine corridors are essential parts of Metro Vancouver's image. They are often conduits between communities. Richmond has done a particularly good job with multi-use trails on both arms of the Fraser River, the west dyke trail and the Shell Road rail-to-trail corridor. What would you like in an urban trail system? Wildlife viewing spots? Sites to learn about history and culture? Restrooms? Parks? Places to snack or get drinks? A major recreational centre like the Richmond Olympic Oval? Check and check some more, and for the latter, an especially big cheque!

Look around: Metro Vancouver is a world-leading city in urban "naturescapes" that combine trail systems and facilities. That is what makes a city truly liveable. Metro Vancouver has the opportunity to model an approach that provides alternate ways to commute, wild spaces for education, local parks to keep physically active and habitat for species other than us. When possible, take the opportunity to share your knowledge of urban naturescapes with others who are less aware of them, thereby spreading the understanding of the importance they hold for a healthy society.

Other Area Interests

To extend your day, you may consider Steveston Village and its market on summer Saturdays, or Garry Point Park for a picnic dinner.

Cycling on the Richmond dyke in spring
(PHOTO COURTESY OF TOURISM RICHMOND)

Vancouver Seawall: Canada Place to Kits Pool

Distance: 42 km
Time: 2.5 – 3.5 hrs.
Level: moderate
Grade: easy < 25 m
Public Transit Route: SkyTrain/Canada Line
Surface: paved

Activity Highlight

If you're like me, when you think of an image of Vancouver, you think of this: a city skyline surrounded by a seawall. It's a sunny day and you stand in a light breeze that forms whitecaps on the ocean. A multicultural diversity of people are playing, conversing, smiling, exercising and drinking coffee on patios of outdoor cafes. How's that? Is it similar to your image? That's what you can expect on this spectacular ride following almost every major landmark that borders the water in central Vancouver: Canada Place, Coal Harbour, Brockton and Prospect points, English Bay, False Creek, Science World, Olympic Village, Granville Island and Kits Beach! Today is the day.

Directions

Begin at Waterfront Station at Canada Place and cycle on the seawall through Coal Harbour, around Stanley Park, English Bay, False Creek, Granville Island and to the west side of Kits Beach. This is a 25.5-km trip one-way. Return the same way until you reach English Bay and then turn right on Park Lane (at the tennis courts and the Vancouver Park Board office). This will take you to Lost Lagoon and back to the seawall leading to Coal Harbour and Waterfront Station. The return trip is 16.5 km long, since you don't go around Stanley Park a second time.

Notes

Maps: For this ride, the maps include the City of Vancouver Cycling Map and the Stanley Park Map. Both are available at City Hall or at the Tourism Vancouver Visitor Centre.

Restrooms: These are available at various places along the route. Remember, you can only go around Stanley Park in one direction on a bike, counter-clockwise, so factor this into your ride.

Safety: This activity is mostly on the seawall, but because of the potential crowds of people, know your safety skills and signs for riding. Clearly communicate your intentions to others while cycling around large numbers of people. In fact, you will find a bell on your bike to be very useful.

Timing: This is a cycling trip to do on a weekday or in the winter due to how busy this area can be.

Company: Get to know this route for when you have visitors in town and you want to share in an active experience with them. There are many rental businesses for bikes in town.

Dogs: Bringing Rover along is not advised due to the urban street cycling with this activity.

Approaching Siwash Rock, also known by the Squamish Nation as Slhx̱i7lsh, on the Stanley Park seawall.

Of Interest: You can cut this ride short when you come out of English Bay, just past Sunset Beach, by taking the Aquabus across to Granville Island at the south end of Hornby Street where it meets False Creek. This cuts off the ride to the end of False Creek where Science World is.

Another option on this route is to combine the seawall around Stanley Park with a ride on the inner trails in the park. One option is to cycle the seawall to just before the Lions Gate Bridge and Prospect Point. Ride, or walk, as it is steep, up the Avision Trail to take in Prospect Point from the top. Cycle down the road 50 m to the Siwash Trail and take it down to Merilees and Third Beach. This will add some elevation to your ride, but the view over the Lions Gate Bridge and from Prospect Point, looking toward Ambleside in West Vancouver, is fantastic.

When in Stanley Park, watch for information signs written by the Stanley Park Ecology Society (SPES) on cultural, historical and natural topics. Completed in 2010, they were part of the remediation money after the 2008 windstorm that greatly affected the park.

Eco-Insight: Stanley Park Ecology Society

David Orr, a distinguished professor of environmental studies in Ohio and a well-known environmentalist, wrote in his book, *Earth in Mind* (1994), that all education is environmental education. He meant that everything we learn has implications on the planet, for better or worse. The SPES provides important environmental education to city and sub-urban dwellers who collectively are becoming more removed from the natural world. This nonprofit leads many stewardship activities and engages thousands by expanding their awareness of the natural world, using Stanley Park as a backdrop. SPES is responsible for a majority of the signs around the park, covering topics from Siwash Rock to local trees. Its education programs range from immersing local youth in urban wilderness camping to taking tourists on nature discovery walks. The society has a young naturalist club, provides monitoring and updates on nesting herons and eagles and empowers communities in co-existing with urban coyotes. They operate Vancouver's only nature centre – on Lost Lagoon – provide elementary schools with field and classroom programming and even run the award-winning Cob House during Halloween and Christmas miniature train events in the park, selling organically grown popcorn to raise thousands for education and conservation projects.

SPES single-handedly enables tens of thousands of people each year to value the natural world and the systems it provides us. There are so many ways an urban dweller can get involved with SPES, such as with habitat restoration, invasive plant removals, beach clean-ups, wildlife and habitat monitoring, public outreach, EcoRanger roving park ambassadors, Nature House hosting, research and data mapping, social media, and school programs. SPES is truly a model organization for urban environmental education. If you ever have reason to look for a cause to celebrate, look no further than SPES in Vancouver.

Other Area Interests

SPES and the Stanley Park Nature House regularly have programs on the go. If you don't know about them, I highly recommend checking out what they are offering at stanleyparkecology.ca.

TOP: *Begin your ride at Canada Place.* (PHOTO COURTESY OF VI JANTZEN)
BOTTOM: *After Stanley Park, English Bay, and BC Place this cycling route passes Science World in False Creek, before continuing to Olympic Village, Granville Island and Kitsilano.*

Fraser Valley Local Food & Wine Tour

Distance: 25 km
Time: 2 – 3 hrs.
Level: easy
Grade: easy < 100 m
Public Transit Routes: 531, C60 – 63
Surface: paved/gravel

Activity Highlight

Roll together a little bit of Tuscany, a smidgen of Okanagan wine country and a dash of Granville Island and what do you have? Well, I don't really know, but it must be something like cycling through markets of local produce, farmers' fields and wine orchards in the Fraser Valley! This recommended activity joins a Slow Food Vancouver bike tour, but if you would rather cycle on your own, read on about Tourism Langley's Circle Farm Route. To learn more about Slow Food, go to slowfoodvancouver.com, while the self-guided Langley route is at circlefarmtour.com/.

Directions

I suggest your first stop is the Slow Food Cycle Tour website at fraservalleycycletours.com and look at its cycle tours for the season you are interested in taking part. The tours are inexpensive, are set up with a shopping shuttle that can carry any items you might purchase (i.e., wine) and are run on days when you can be certain all locations will be open. The tours will give you a better chance to meet the farmers and support the local food movement.

If you choose to cycle Langley's Circle Farm Route on your own, know that opening time and days may vary depending on the season. Check the circlefarmtour.com website for days and times the businesses are open and contact the Langley Chamber of Commerce to ensure you have the most updated map. The map directs you to a variety of specialty farm-gate vendors, open air markets, charming eateries, heritage sites and more. One route option looks like this:

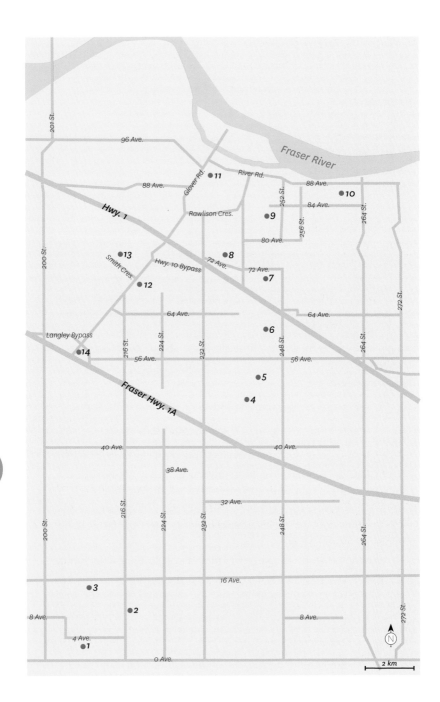

1. Vista D'oro Farms & Winery

2. Domaine de Chaberton Winery and Bacchus Bistro

3. Township 7 Vineyards & Winery

4. Erikson's Daylily Gardens

5. JD Farms Specialty Turkey Store

6. Krause Berry Farms and Estate Winery

7. Thunderbird Equestrian Show Park

8. Driediger Farms Market

9. Aldor Acres Dairy Centre

10. The Fort Wine Company

11. Fort Langley National Historic Site

12. Cedar Rim Nursery

13. Milner Valley Cheese

14. Langley Community Farmers Market

Notes

Restrooms: Most of the farmers retail sites should have restrooms.

Safety: As some of this activity will be on city streets, know your safety skills and signs for riding around vehicles if you have not done this for a while.

Timing: This activity is best done on summer Saturdays between 10:00 am and 4:00 pm, as this is the most likely day and time the farms will be open. Contact the Langley Chamber of Commerce to see if it has anything organized as well.

Dogs: This route is not recommended for dogs due to street cycling, traffic and cycling near farms with animals.

Of Interest: The Slow Food movement has associated cycle tours in many BC communities. A quick web search will turn up others run in the past in Chilliwack, Agassiz, Pemberton, Comox and Sooke. Routes are often flat, not too long and suitable for families.

Eco-Insight: Slow Food Movement & Food Security

What is Slow Food you ask? The Slow Food movement started 25 years ago because founder Carlo Petrini believed that we are on the verge of losing something beautiful, basic and essential to life: the diversity of food, the richness of our traditions and the connection between what we eat and how it is produced. Since then, Slow Food has become the only movement to connect the pleasure of food with social responsibility; fighting for the fundamental right to good, clean and fair food for everyone.

The aim of Slow Food is to connect people to their food and to the food systems (such as small farms) that surround them. Regional cuisine is paramount in Slow Food and the farming of plants and seeds that are characteristic of the local ecosystem is encouraged. "Slow Foodies" believe in genetic diversity of crops, which ensures a large gene pool to draw on. Preserving as many varieties of a species, such

Cyclists learning about Slow Food on farm roads in the Fraser Valley
(PHOTOS COURTESY OF TOURISM CHILLIWACK)

as potato, tomato or corn, is an important objective for the movement. Closing the gap between farm and plate leads to greater food security because we come to rely on our communities, rather than far-flung places, for our nourishment. Metro Vancouver is fortunate to have easy access to a nourishing local land and sea.

In the spring, watch for local spot prawns and halibut – both are caught sustainably in British Columbia. In the summer, Okanagan fruit and Fraser Valley vegetables are plentiful – you can even try u-pick. In the fall, seek out coastal salmon, along with BC grains and nuts. Finally, in the winter, many chards, kale and root vegetables still grow and are available at local farms. Take the time to learn about local food. Eating local is healthy both for you and for the planet. And this Fraser Valley local food and wine cycle is a great way to start!

Other Area Interests

Chances are if you cycle the entire route, you will have had more than enough visiting. However, if you do decide to add an extension to your day, consider Fort Langley – it's worth some extra time while in the Langley area.

Go Further: Lochside Trail from Swartz Bay to Victoria

Distance: 66 km
Time: full day
Level: moderate
Grade: easy < 50 m
Public Transit Route: 620 to the BC Ferries terminal and BC Ferries (Tsawwassen-Swartz Bay) to Vancouver Island
Surface: gravel/paved

Activity Highlight

OMG! I'm over 40, so I don't really know what this means, but I understand from the teenagers in my life that you use it when you're excited about something! It's easy to be excited about the Lochside Trail. This is surely one of the easiest to ride and more spectacular trails close to Vancouver. This bike path is stunning – from an ocean vista ride past Sidney, through dappled sunlit deciduous forest and amid farmers' fields. This trail also has almost no elevation change and ends in downtown Victoria. This is a must-do at some point for your summer cycling excursions.

Directions

Consider parking in Tsawwassen (free parking) and riding your bike to the BC Ferries terminal. Then take BC Ferries from Tsawwassen to Swartz Bay. As you leave the car deck from the ship, ride uphill in the bike lane to the first overpass and turn up and to the right to go on (and over) the overpass. From here, follow the signs for the Lochside Trail. The trail is mostly flat all the way to downtown Victoria.

Notes

Maps: You can find maps and a trail guide online at the Capital Region District website (crd.bc.ca/parks-recreation-culture/commuting-cycling). You can also request a map by mail.

Restrooms: These are about every 10 km on the route.

Safety: Watch for horse riders and hikers on the trail. I found I was blinded when wearing sunglasses and riding from the bright sun to a strongly tree-shaded part of the trail.

Timing: All times of year are suitable for this ride as long as you are wearing the proper clothing.

Company: This is an especially good activity to take visitors on if they are active and interested in seeing Victoria.

Dogs: Rover must be on-leash while on the trail.

Of Interest: While cycling the Lochside, consider a stop at Michell's Farm Market at the Island View Road crossing and at the Blenkinsop Trestle before getting into Victoria.

Both the #70 and #72 buses travel between Victoria and Swartz Bay, so if you plan to have a few drinks on, say, the Sticky Wicket rooftop patio in downtown Victoria, and are not up for the return ride, then take a transit bus with bike racks. Note bus racks only take two bikes per bus. This cycle is a fun one-way excursion as well. A good stop on your return trip, if you aren't rushing for the ferry, is the aquarium in Sidney. The elevation on this trip is mostly due to climbing up overpasses coming out of Swartz Bay or downtown Victoria. Otherwise, this is a flat trail.

Eco-Insight: Douglas Fir Forest

As you cycle the Lochside Trail, notice how the forest differs from the forests of Metro Vancouver. British Columbia has 14 biogeoclimatic zones; that is, zones where the bio (life), geo (earth) and climate (long-term weather) all combine to create distinct conditions that support different assemblages of plants and animals. For example, in Vancouver, the coastal western hemlock reigns supreme, but where you are on the island, in British Columbia's smallest biogeoclimatic zone, the Douglas fir is the most common tree. This makes a big difference to the biodiversity in these two areas because as dominant tree species

OPPOSITE: *Fall leaves on the Lochside Trail*

TOP: *While riding along the ocean's edge, watch for oystercatchers – crow-sized birds with what appear to be orange straws attached to their heads.*

BOTTOM: *Black-tailed deer are abundant on southern Vancouver Island.*

(PHOTO COURTESY OF ROB ALEXANDER)

change, so do many of the species surrounding them. Although there is species overlap between the mainland and southeastern Vancouver Island, there are also substantial differences. Southeastern Vancouver Island is in a rain shadow, meaning it experiences more sun, less rain, milder temperatures and longer summer seasons. Its soil is sandier and its biology includes rare plants and even trees (such as Garry oak) not seen in Metro Vancouver. If you are cycling the trail in summer, try to identify the following species on your ride:

- *Douglas fir* – a tall tree with very thick, deeply furrowed bark and light-green needles;
- *grand fir* – a tall, straight tree with flat, dark-green needles that alternate long and short;
- *Garry oak* – a deciduous tree that has deeply furrowed bark but with oak leaves;
- *arbutus* – an evergreen, broadleaf tree with peeling red bark revealing smooth, green bark underneath; bent and sinewy trunks; leaves that drop all year;
- *flowering dogwood* – a deciduous tree that flowers in the spring and sometimes early fall; our provincial tree, protected by law;
- *salal* – a shrub with dark-green, thick, round leaves used in floral arrangements; berries are edible in late August;
- *Oregon grape* – a low shrub with holly-like leaves; yellow flowers turn to milky blue berries;
- *wild rose* – pink flowering fragrant shrubs.

Other Area Interests

If you like this activity, then try the Galloping Goose Regional Trail from Victoria to Sooke next time. After that, take the ferry from Sidney to San Juan Island and ride there. So much to do!

Paddling

"If there is magic on the planet, it is contained in water."

—Loren Eiseley, American Scientist, 1907 – 1977

Vancouver is a coastal city and to experience it only by land is, well, it's limiting. Kayaking and canoeing are the paddler's main choices (although paddleboarding is gaining in popularity), but our heritage frequently creates a preference. Those from central Canada often prefer one, while those born and bred in British Columbia prefer the other. Can you guess who prefers which? Both boats, however, allow you to access locations difficult to reach, or unreachable, by land. There are many other reasons to try a water activity. Kayaking and canoeing are both easy to learn and provide you with the ability to explore an environment at close proximity. Whether that is a narrow side channel or an lowwater tide pool, they give you the ability to move quietly, explore and enjoy the natural world if you choose. Both build upper body muscle, but brute strength is not necessary for either as both are more about technique and balance. Finally, because kayaks and canoes

The Vancouver shoreline is a beautiful evening paddle, but don't forget the proper lighting and reflective gear to ensure you are seen by other boats. (PHOTO COURTESY OF LORI GEOSITS)

are so quiet, they enable paddlers to socialize as they go. This chapter provides ideas to inspire you to get on the water this year, and there is no time like the present.

All six activities covered in this chapter are for those who may not have access to their own boat. In the summer, rentals (kayaks and/ or canoes) are available at or near Buntzen Lake, Widgeon Slough, Belcarra Park, Granville Island and Deep Cove. In addition, kayak companies will bring a rental kayak to the Nicomekl River for you to paddle. These paddling activities cover a range of water types. While the Belcarra, Vancouver shoreline and Deep Cove activities are on the ocean, the Nicomekl is a freshwater river that feeds into Boundary Bay. Buntzen is a lake overseen by BC Hydro, while the paddle to Widgeon crosses the outlet of a lake (Pitt Lake) and remains in a slow-flowing slough.

Plan for safety just as you would with hiking. Follow the Safety & Security Planning section in this book, along with the ten activity safety essentials and the Safety Equipment Specific for Water Activities, to prepare properly for your paddle. Have a plan for your paddle and know your limits and the limits of those paddling with you. Moreover, know the forecasted weather, particularly the winds, as well as the tides and currents. Learning paddling inevitably means studying and understanding the environmental conditions to ensure safety.

Paddling is yet another sport that can take you through a lifetime. It's easy to include others, especially those who may not have the opportunity to get out on their own. Children, teenagers, older adults or people with disabilities are all groups to think of when looking for a partner on the water. There are numerous kayak clubs and associations to learn skills, obtain certification or become part of a community sharing in the sport. One word of advice is to access the knowledge of those communities before committing to purchasing big items such as boats. Those with experience on the water understand the nuances of watercraft and utilizing their expertise will help you make better decisions.

The Vancouver Shoreline

Distance: 5 – 13 km
Time: 2 – 5 hrs.
Level: easy
Water Conditions: moderate wind and waves
Public Transit Route: SkyTrain/Canada Line

Activity Highlight

It would be difficult to find a more urban paddle than False Creek to English Bay in Vancouver's West End. However, if you are looking for a West Coast urban kayak experience, this is it! It's easy to see why Vancouver consistently rates as one of the world's most attractive coastal cities when one views it by the water. There are numerous locations to dock your kayak and you may find you are out of the water as much as you are on it!

Directions

You can choose your direction and paddle one, two or all three routes. The three routes are: 1) Granville Island into False Creek and Science World (5.5-km return); 2) Granville Island to English Bay and Second Beach (5.5-km return); and 3) Granville Island to the pier on the far side of Kits Beach (5-km return). A combination of the three provides a 13-km return paddle. See the safety comments in the Notes regarding the water traffic in this busy area.

Notes

Maps: A downtown Vancouver map with the waterfront on it should be adequate to orient you. These are located at the Tourism Vancouver Visitor Centre and most downtown hotels.

Restrooms: These are located at Granville Island and at all of the beaches.

Safety: This is a busy area with commercial traffic, pleasure boaters, False Creek ferries and Aquabus ferries. Guarantee there is lots

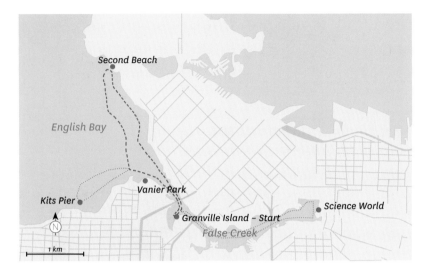

of space around you when paddling and ensure your awareness of boat traffic is vigilant. Don't forget your PFDs and pay attention to the weather as the wind can make it difficult to paddle at times.

Timing: If you plan to paddle near dusk or dawn, be sure to have proper lighting on your boat.

Company: If you have visitors coming to Vancouver, this is a great introduction to the city. Alternately, if you are a visitor yourself, find a local who would like to be a "tourist in their own town" and ask them to join you.

Dogs: Canine companions are not appropriate for this activity.

Of Interest: It's worth noting the sites a shoreline paddle like this can access. These include Granville Island; Vanier Park (including Vancouver Museum, H.R. MacMillan Space Centre and Bard on the Beach); Sunset, Second and Kitsilano beaches; English Bay; Vancouver's West End; False Creek; Science World; Olympic Village and David Lam Park.

Rentals: Kayaks are available for rent on Granville Island, the suggested starting point for this paddle.

TOP: *Orcas are an iconic BC species.* (PHOTO COURTESY OF TERRY BEREZAN)
BOTTOM: *City kayaking in Vancouver often means being dwarfed by towering condos.*

Eco-Insight: Orcas

Look around the city for symbols of the orca – the Vancouver Canucks logo, the Vancouver Aquarium's bronze statue by Bill Reid and the Lego-looking orca sculpture by Douglas Coupland at the Vancouver Convention Centre are examples. The orca (killer whale) is a fixture in Metro Vancouver and arguably the most popular marine mammal on the West Coast. We have three separate types of orca (which is a dolphin species, not a true whale) in British Columbia. The Eco-Insights in this book are about discovering connections and I'd like to provide one set of connections for each type of BC orca: residents, transients and offshores.

Resident orcas, often seen in larger pods, eat salmon and strongly prefer chinook, even where other salmon species are more abundant. The predator-prey relationship is so tight that when the numbers of chinook rise or fall, so, too, does the number of resident killer whales. Interestingly, in low-chinook years, orcas don't alter their diet but instead spend more energy looking further for their prey.

Transient orcas eat marine mammals such as seals and often travel alone. However, there is one location along the West Coast where transient orcas congregate. Just off Alaska's Unimak Island, scientists have seen approximately 150 transient killer whales lying in wait for grey whales migrating from Baja, CA, with their new calves. For at least a month, these orcas feed exclusively on the whale calves.

Offshore orcas live near the edge of the continental shelf and prey on Pacific sleeper sharks. This shark's skin is so abrasive it is thought to wear the whales' teeth flat. By old age, it is believed that younger whales, whose teeth are still functional, may share their own prey with their dentally challenged elders.

Other Area Interests

Plan to spend additional time in this area with a visit to some of Vancouver's main attractions: Science World and its Omnimax theatre, Vancouver Museum, H.R. MacMillan Space Centre, Granville Island or Vancouver's beaches.

Buntzen Lake Paddle to the North End

Distance: 6 – 7 km
Time: 1.5 – 2.5 hrs.
Level: easy
Water Conditions: moderate wind and waves
Public Transit Routes: 190, C26 "Buntzen Lake Special" (see Notes)

Activity Highlight

Do you have access to a canoe and do you like getting up early for an adventure? If so, this is a great paddle for carrying breakfast and a thermos of coffee to North Beach on Buntzen Lake for an early weekend adventure. It's short enough to do with kids and can be completed before the mid-day crowds. Also, it can be combined with trail walking or swimming from the North Beach dock.

Directions

Launch your canoe or kayak from the South Beach boat launch at Buntzen Lake. The paddle to North Beach is straight. You can add extra mileage by venturing around the islands at the south end, by paddling south to the boardwalk after your launch and by exploring the shoreline on the west side of the lake.

Notes

Transit & Transportation: The #190 bus will get you to Coquitlam Centre, and the C26 "Buntzen Lake Special" gets you to Buntzen Lake, however, the Buntzen Lake Special is a summer-only bus.

Maps: Buntzen Lake maps are available both onsite and online at the BC Hydro Recreation Areas website (bchydro.com/community/recreation_areas/buntzen_lake.html).

Restrooms: These are located at both the north and south ends of the lake.

Safety: Don't forget your PFDs and pay attention to the weather as the wind can make it difficult to paddle at times. Buntzen Lake is cold

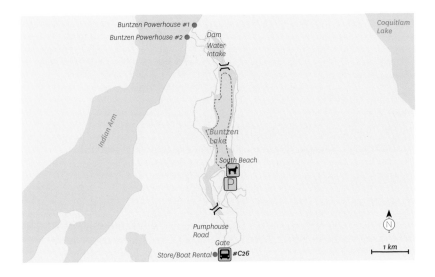

and it can literally take your breath away when jumping in. Splash your face and upper body first to adapt your body to the water's temperature. Also, read the "Safety around Water" section on the Buntzen Lake website provided above.

Timing: If you plan to spend time on the lake in the evening, note the time the park gate closes. It is (really) bad karma to be in your boat at North Beach, with your car in the south parking area and the security guard having to wait for you to return before closing the gate for the night.

Company: Instead of meeting a friend at your local coffee shop on a summer weekend, fill a thermos with coffee, pack some fruit and croissants and entice them to join you for breakfast at Buntzen. If you know kids who could use some outside time, this is a perfect activity for them too.

Dogs: Rover must be on-leash when out of the boat and on the trails. An off-leash area is located at the south end of the lake next to the parking area.

Of Interest: Buntzen Lake is a reservoir and is used to control the water flow to the Buntzen Power Station on Indian Arm. Large pipes funnel water from the lake down a steep incline to the power generators

My sons Christopher taking up the bow position and Brent jumping off the dock after our paddle to the north end of Buntzen Lake.

A bear eating a spawned salmon and the beginning of another amazing cycle of life. (PHOTO COURTESY OF JENN DICKIE)

160 m below. The inflow to the lake comes from a 3.6-km-long tunnel that cuts through the mountain from Coquitlam Lake.

Rentals: There is a store just before the Buntzen Lake gate that rents boats (in the summer) if you do not have your own.

Eco-Insight: Bears, Salmon & Temperate Forests

Earlier, in the PoCo trail Eco-Insight (see page 154), I discussed salmon spawning in the Coquitlam River and suggested that energy from the salmon may feed an ecosystem you wouldn't have guessed. Energy comes to ecosystems in many ways but always at the foundation is energy from the sun, which is transferred to plants through the process of photosynthesis. When animals eat the plants, and then other animals eat those animals, that energy is passed along the food chain. Tom Reimchen, a professor of biology and ecology at the University of Victoria, carried out research on ways energy is transferred in ecosystems in Haida Gwaii (the Queen Charlotte Islands off coastal British Columbia) and he discovered a fascinating link. The broker in that link is the bear.

Tom Reimchen's work focused on relationships, specifically relationships between black bears, salmon and the forest surrounding a stream. One way the bears avoid competition while feeding is by taking the salmon they catch away from the stream and into the forest. Tom noticed that enormous trees surround the areas where an abundance of half-eaten carcasses, carried into the forest by bears, remained to rot. Martens, eagles, ravens, gulls, beetles and fly larvae scavenge the salmon left on the forest floor. He wondered if the marine nutrients contained in the salmon, originally from the open ocean, could be feeding trees as well as the scavengers. His research showed that in six weeks of spawning, each bear caught about 700 fish, leaving half of each carcass in the forest. At 2.2 kg per fish, this amounts to 120 kg of fish fertilizer per hectare of land in the area each year. British Columbia's 100,000 bears could be transferring 60 million kilograms of salmon tissue annually into the rainforest.

Salmon flesh contains an ocean-abundant nitrogen isotope (N15) that is rarer on land. By taking sample cores from trees next to the stream and studying these in a lab, Tom discovered that rings grown in the years when salmon were more abundant had higher concentrations of N15. This helps connect historical trends in salmon abundance with yearly growth rings in trees – amazing!

Other Area Interests

If time permits, tie up your boat and take a walk from North Beach along the trails to the Buntzen Powerhouse on Indian Arm. This is an important historical building and offers a great view of Indian Arm.

Deep Cove Crossing to Belcarra Regional Park

Distance: 6 km
Time: 2 – 3 hrs.
Level: moderate
Water Conditions: moderate wind, waves and current
Public Transit Routes: 211, 212, C15

Activity Highlight

Name two parks in Metro Vancouver separated in distance by 2.8 km (as the crow flies) but 49 km by road. Panorama Park in Deep Cove and Belcarra Park in Port Moody fit this scenario. If you are proficient on the water (see Notes), launch a rented boat from Deep Cove, located on Indian Arm, and paddle in a backwards S, 2.8 km to Port Moody. Belcarra and Deep Cove each have their own charm. The former is

(PHOTO COURTESY OF VALERIE BELANGER)

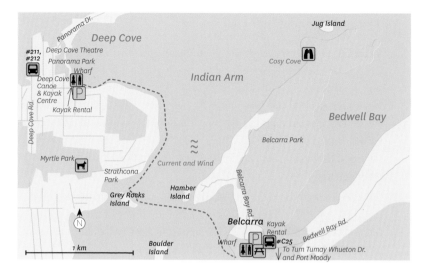

popular for fishing and crabbing, while the latter is a recreational hub of sailing, kayaking, canoeing, paddleboarding and swimming.

Directions

I would recommend beginning this trip at Deep Cove as it's a protected area, allowing you to gauge your (or your group's) ability before travelling into more open water. It is also slightly easier to launch a boat from Deep Cove than from Belcarra. If you follow the shoreline and cross to Belcarra, the trip will be about 2.8 km each way.

Notes

Maps: I suggest printing satellite maps for this area from Google Maps or acquiring a marine chart.

Restrooms: These are located at the launch area in both Deep Cove and in Belcarra Park.

Safety: I can't stress the importance of the advice given in this safety section enough; please consider it carefully. Don't forget your PFDS and pay attention to the weather, as the wind during the crossing of Indian Arm to Belcarra can be strong. Be sure to know if the tide is coming in or going out. Follow the shoreline and then cross at the narrow point across from Hamber Island. Be aware that the current is strongest between Hamber and Grey Rocks (about one knot). Be sure to watch for boat traffic coming from multiple directions. The inflow wind from the south can get quite strong, especially on a sunny summer afternoon. Paddle carefully along the right (south) shore as you leave Deep Cove and test the wind before you turn right, rounding the corner toward Hamber Island. If in doubt, ask for advice from the staff at Deep Cove Canoe & Kayak. They would be very willing to help you. Read the additional safety information in the introduction to this chapter and book.

Do you know how to do a self-rescue in a kayak? If not, consider taking a course at Deep Cove or Ecomarine Paddlesport Centres (ecomarine.com) on Granville Island before attempting crossings such as this one of Indian Arm.

Timing: Spring through fall is the best time for this paddle. Be sure to check out the tide tables at tides-marees.gc.ca before you go.

Company: Paddle with someone who has some experience on the water, since Indian Arm can be windy, has a moderate current and can be busy with boating traffic.

Dogs: Furry friends should be on-leash when out of your boat at both ends. Deep Cove's closest designated off-leash area is at Myrtle Park.

Of Interest: This activity includes an additional paddle south to Grey Rocks Island, but if you did not do this, you could eliminate one kilometre of this adventure – but why would you want to do that? There is a nice park called Strathcona near Grey Rocks.

Rentals: You can rent kayaks at both Deep Cove and Belcarra.

Eco-Insight: Fostering Awareness & Curiosity

During your paddle between Deep Cove and Belcarra, it is likely you will observe various birds, possibly a mammal and an array of plants and trees. The following excerpt is from an important, local, natural history book called *BC: A Natural History*, by Sydney and Richard Cannings (Vancouver: Greystone Books, 1996). On page five they write:

TOP: *Fostering curiosity...do you know what this is?* (PHOTO COURTESY OF ROB ALEXANDER)

BOTTOM: *Watch for mature and juvenile eagles on the water or in the trees.* (PHOTO COURTESY OF RORRI MCBLANE)

The very diversity that makes the natural world fascinating can also make it an intimidating subject to study…Studying natural history is also a lot like learning a foreign language. A few guidebooks are necessary to act as dictionaries, frequent practice is a good idea, and it really helps to have friends who are fluent in the subject…It helps to learn the names of at least the common trees and shrubs if you want to understand the forest's basic ecology…knowing the names leads to other discoveries…After you can answer the simple "What is it?"…you are ready to go on to the much more interesting questions of where, how, why and when. You are ready to read the landscape, meaning that you keep your eyes and the rest of your senses open for patterns and continually ask yourself questions…Reading the landscape means you can never get bored outside again – it turns every hike and drive into a learning adventure.

The concept of "reading the landscape" resonates with me because, in addition to learning, fostering awareness and curiosity about the world around us is paramount if we are to live sustainably in this rapidly changing world. Perhaps today is the day you begin questioning.

Other Area Interests

Deep Cove has a quaint theatre run by Deep Cove Stage Society. It offers an array of events. I have always wanted to do an evening paddle (with headlamps and safety gear) from Belcarra to Deep Cove for dinner and a theatre performance, then kayak back later in the evening. I have yet to do this, but if someone does, please let me know how the evening goes – it seems like the quintessential West Coast date night!

Deep Cove Crossing to Jug Island

Distance: 5.5 km
Time: 2 – 3 hrs.
Level: moderate
Water Conditions: moderate wind, waves and current
Public Transit Routes: 211, 212, C15

Activity Highlight

Indian Arm is a jewel in Metro Vancouver, but without access to a boat, it's difficult to experience. So how do you explore this glacial fjord easily? If you are proficient on the water (see Notes), then launch a rented boat from Deep Cove. Deep Cove Canoe & Kayak (deepcovekayak .com) has many options for gear and safety equipment and offers instruction as well. A short trip to Jug Island and a secluded beach facing it is a perfect introduction to this popular area. On weekdays, it is likely you will have this entire area to yourself. Surely, access to water like this must be one reason we live and play in a coastal city like Vancouver!

Directions

On weekends, Deep Cove Canoe & Kayak can be busy launching many boats of their own, so be aware of this potentially busy area. Follow the shoreline out of the cove and cross Indian Arm in a straight line (about 1 km), then follow the shoreline north, where you round the tip to the right and see Jug Island in front of you. There is a beach to pull out on for a great picnic spot. Minimize loitering in the middle of the channel where there is boat traffic, but linger as much as you want on the edges of this paddle.

Notes

Maps: I suggest printing satellite maps for this area from Google Maps or acquiring a marine chart.

Restrooms: These are located at the launch area in Deep Cove and at

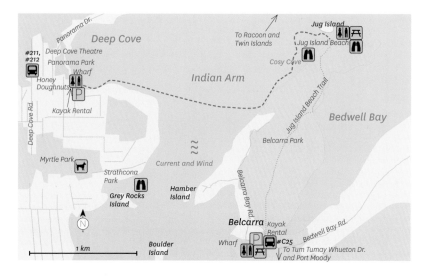

Jug Island Beach. I suggest you bring your own toilet paper – you can't rely on the outhouse to be stocked!

Community art in Deep Cove

Safety: I can't stress the importance of the advice in this safety section enough, so please consider it carefully. Don't forget your PFDs and pay attention to the weather as the wind during the crossing of Indian Arm can be moderately, or even very, strong. Be sure to know if the tide is coming in or going out. Watch for boat traffic, and if you go in the evening, have good lighting systems in place for twilight and after sunset. The inflow wind from the south can get quite strong, especially on a sunny summer afternoon. Paddle carefully along the right (south) shore as you leave Deep Cove and test the wind before you go out into Indian Arm. If in doubt, ask for advice from the staff at Deep Cove Canoe & Kayak. They are very willing to help.

Do you know how to do a self-rescue in a kayak? If not, consider taking a course at Deep Cove or Ecomarine Paddlesports Centres (ecomarine.com) on Granville Island before attempting crossings such as this one of Indian Arm.

Timing: Spring through fall is the best time for this paddle. Be sure to check out the tide tables at tides-marees.gc.ca before you go.

Company: Do you have active visitors who would like an ocean adventure? This may be a good day trip to do with them if you consider yourselves intermediate in your abilities on the water.

Dogs: Your best friend should be on a leash when out of your boat at both ends of this paddle. Deep Cove's closest designated off-leash area is at Myrtle Park.

Of Interest: An additional paddle north to Raccoon Island and then to Twin Islands (where there is a campsite for a future overnight excursion) adds an additional 5.75 total kilometres to the adventure.

Eco-Insight: Water Temperature, Acidity & Species Diversity

Recordings of CO_2 levels in our atmosphere hit 400 parts per million (ppm) in 2013. The pre-industrial average was 278 ppm, and in 1979, it was only 336 ppm. The global temperature increase over the past 50 years was 0.75°C, and the rise toward the poles was even higher. According to scientists, even if emissions are capped at today's levels, lag time (the time for the earth's systems to reach equilibrium levels) ensures several more decades of rising CO_2 levels and therefore higher temperatures. Given that, our national conversation must turn to mitigation and adaptation rather than just prevention; however, when electing our governments, it seems we sometimes ignore climate concerns and focus instead on economic agendas, worrying our standard of living will decrease. Climate change has become political, but it shouldn't be. The environment that supports us transcends politics, and, ultimately, the state of our atmosphere and oceans will define living standards here and around the globe. Atmospheric and oceanic conditions relate directly to the conditions of our future.

As you prepare to paddle in the spectacular surroundings of Deep Cove, also consider the state of the ocean. Just like the atmosphere, the ocean is warming. As it warms, the water expands, and ocean levels rise, putting at risk low-lying islands. (Consider that a rise of only a couple of metres would submerge Jug Island and many of the lower islands in Howe Sound.) Approximately 85 per cent of the earth's CO_2 is captured by the ocean, while the atmosphere contains only 3 per cent. (The remaining approximately 12 per cent is stored in rocks, such as limestone, in the earth's crust.) As it absorbs CO_2 from the atmosphere, the ocean is becoming increasingly acidic, and this acidity affects many species for which it is home, especially those that form calcium carbonate shells or corals. Recall from your elementary school science experiment how vinegar dissolves eggshells or baking soda (sodium bicarbonate – a similar compound to seashells), releasing the trapped CO_2 as bubbles. A similar fate awaits many ocean species as ocean acidity increases. Ultimately, acidity will affect global food supplies and the extinction of many ocean species will certainly follow.

The environment trumps the economy – hands down! Our complacency will cause pain for future generations. We must wake up!

Other Area Interests

Honey Doughnuts & Goodies is a popular place to get last-minute, sugar-infused baking prior to your canoe or kayak departure. Jug Island beach also has a trail that connects with the main part of Belcarra Park (approximately one hour each way), if you want to stretch your legs.

Kayaks at sunset (PHOTO COURTESY OF VALERIE BELANGER)

Nicomekl Lazy River Paddle

Distance: 8 – 17.5 km
Time: 3 – 5 hrs.
Level: easy
Water Conditions: mild wind and waves
Public Transit Routes: 351, 375

Activity Highlight

With the word "lazy" in the title of this activity, you can imagine how easy this paddle is. It's also an indication that your plan for today is not an adrenaline rush. This is simply a lovely soft-adventure float down Nicomekl River. However, this activity does provide multiple take-out points to extend your experience and add more mileage. The river meanders past farmers' fields, forest edges, suburban mansions and, ultimately, to the river beaches at Blackie Spit. You may not expend the calories you will gain eating ice cream in Crescent Beach when you are done, but you can balance that out next time!

Directions

There are two entrances to Elgin Heritage Park—one at Historic Stewart Farm, just east of 136th Street, and the other just west of 136th Street, leading to a large open parking area. From the dock or boat ramp at Historic Stewart Farm, you can easily launch a kayak or canoe on the Nicomekl River. At Elgin Road, 2 km east of your put in point, there is a small one-way car and foot bridge (which happens to be a dam). You can't canoe under it, so it requires a 100-metre portage over Elgin Road if you are to continue upriver. Watch for cars coming over the bridge as they *will not* be expecting a boat carried by paddlers crossing their path. The water flow below this dam is affected by the tide but rarely has a strong flow in either direction. Above the dam, there is slightly more westward flow of water in the spring, compared to summer or fall, however it is easy to paddle in both directions on this river as you glide under railway trestles and road bridges.

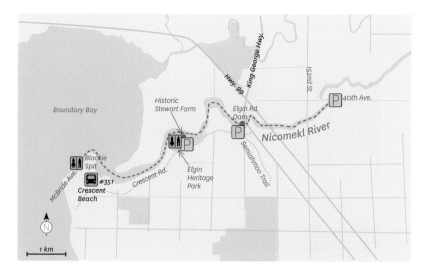

Depending on your planned time and distance, your route options may look like this:

- Elgin Park dock west to Blackie Spit and the Crescent Beach boat launch (located at the end of McBride Avenue at the Surrey Sailing Club) – 8-km return;

- Elgin Park dock east to bridge/dam at Elgin Road – 4-km return;

- dam at Elgin Road to 40th Avenue bridge – 5.5-km return.

If you have access to a driver to drop you off and pick you up, then another option is to paddle one way, starting at the 40th Avenue bridge and paddle 1.5 – 2 hours to Crescent Beach. There are walking trails that parallel the river between the Historic Stewart Farm and Elgin Road for your shuttle driver to wander while they wait for you.

Notes

Maps: Besides the map in this book, I suggest printing satellite maps for this area from Google Maps.

Restrooms: These are located at the launch site at Historic Stewart Farm in Elgin Park only.

Timing: Places to pull out on the river for a break or picnic may be rare

TOP: *Starting a Christmas day paddle with my father-in-law Dick on the Nicomekl at the 40th Avenue bridge.*
BOTTOM: *The Nicomekl offers a number of opportunities to paddle under bridges, including this railway trestle.*

(PHOTOS COURTESY OF HEATHER AVISON)

depending on the season. There are several bridges you paddle under and most have a place to take a break or get shade.

Company: Do you know someone with a canoe in their backyard that never sees the light of day or the "spray of the sea"? Perhaps asking them to join you with their boat for a slack, summer-day paddle is in order.

Dogs: Canines could be good company in a canoe and are sure to enjoy a river dip.

Of Interest: Watch for eagles, hawks, owls, herons, kingfishers, ducks and shorebirds throughout your paddle.

On your paddle by Elgin Heritage Park, watch for the orange buoys in the river. The distance from the eastern-most buoy is 2000 m, precisely, to the western-most one. These are used by the Nicomekl Rowing Club for races.

The high banks of the river will shield most of the fields you pass. If the opportunity arises, stop the boat, climb the bank and look around – this is some of the most fertile land in Western Canada.

At the Elgin Road bridge/dam, the river crosses the Semiahmoo Trail, originally an Aboriginal travel-way linking First Nations villages in the south to the Fraser River's prolific salmon grounds to the north. This trail later became the Semiahmoo Wagon Road, which was a key part to opening the Surrey we know today.

Eco-Insight: Fraser River Delta

The Fraser River drains over 200,000 square kilometres of British Columbia. From the Continental Divide in Mount Robson Provincial Park, beyond Prince George to the north, Kemano to the west and Kamloops in the interior, this river funnels both water and sediment toward Metro Vancouver. After draining more than one-quarter of the province, the Fraser River empties into the Strait of Georgia at the delta's leading edge, depositing 20 million tonnes of sediment into the Pacific Ocean annually. Over thousands of years, this sediment has built up, forming the delta we see today. Its floodplains provide rich farmland, while its wetlands are important stopover locations for migrating shorebirds. According to the Canadian Heritage Rivers System

(CHRS), the Fraser River basin produces more salmon than any other river system in the world! It also holds record-sized sturgeon, provides water to important resource and commercial operations that line it and, of course, is the backyard to most of British Columbia's population.

It's useful to connect the dots in this system. Consider that water, sediment and the nutrients they carry cross the province and create land that is a base for our food supply. That rich farmland produces blueberries and strawberries in the summer; cranberries, pumpkins and potatoes in the fall; and chard and kale throughout the year. Upon consumption, their nutrients transfer from the plants to our bodies and the calories power our paddle through the Nicomekl. Ted Perry, a scriptwriter, wrote a stirring quote in 1971 (though it has since been attributed to Chief Seattle): "This we know: All things are connected like the blood that unites us. We did not weave the web of life; we are merely a strand in it. Whatever we do to the web, we do to ourselves." Food for thought.

Other Area Interests

Spend some extra time getting to know Blackie Spit and Crescent Beach if the area is new to you. There are many short, but attractive, trails in this south section of Surrey. Of course, White Rock Pier is worth a visit as well, but be certain to have money for the parking meters as attendants there are diligent in ensuring spots are paid for.

Go Further: Widgeon Slough & Falls at Pitt Lake

Distance: 9 – 15 km
Time: 4 – 6 hrs.
Level: moderate
Water Conditions: moderate wind, waves and tide
Public Transit Routes: no transit

Activity Highlight

Are you looking for a water-based activity that will take a full day? Do you have access to a canoe or kayak? Do you like to explore? If you answered each of these questions in the affirmative, and are proficient on the water, then this activity is for you. In the spring, water will be rushing fast over Widgeon Falls. In the summer, you'll want to play in the water. In the autumn, salmon will be darting back and forth under your boat. Pick your season and expect it to be among your most memorable paddle experiences of the year.

Directions

Begin this activity at the Grant Narrows Regional Park boat launch. The most difficult, and potentially the most dangerous, part of this paddle is at the start. You need to canoe due west across Pitt Lake, often across the prevailing wind, and across the path of motorboats speeding by. The crossing will take about 15 minutes at full paddle. Once at the mouth of Widgeon Slough, you can relax and meander as you head north and west to a BC Forest Service campsite. From there you can pull your boat out of the water, tie it off and hike a trail to Widgeon Falls. While in the boat, pay attention to the tides because at low tide you may have to get out of your canoe and line it across the shallows as you approach Widgeon Creek. When you get to a T-junction (at about 30 minutes), go left. The paddle to the end is a calm 4.5 km each way, while the walk to the falls is an undulating 3 km each way, with a 50-m elevation change. About 200 m into the hike, veer right to hike along

the river. I suggest taking the time to do both, as the falls are a beautiful place to spend a summer's day.

Notes

Maps: I suggest printing satellite maps for this area from Google Maps.

Restrooms: These are located at the launch area at Pitt Lake and at the start of your hike to Widgeon Falls (the pit toilets are part of a BC Forest Service campsite).

Safety: Remember your PFDs and pay attention to the weather. The wind during the crossing of Pitt Lake to the slough can be strong.

Timing: The lake and slough are tidal, so this may factor into your timing. You will notice this as you paddle with, or against, the tide. This also means that if the tide is going out, the water may get low enough that you have to get out of the boat and push because the boat is touching the bottom. On the other hand, if the tide is coming in, and your boat isn't up high enough on land at the campsite, you may find your boat taken out by the tide when you return from your hike. *Be sure to pull your boat up high enough on land, tie it to something and know if the tide is coming in or going out.* Tide tables can be found at tides-marees.gc.ca. From the New Westminster tide station times, add

4 – 6 hours for tides at Grant Narrows. The West Coast Paddler website (westcoastpaddler.com) has more information.

Company: This is a great trip to do with teenagers or children as it offers an easy paddle. In low water, kids have fun getting out of the boat and walking in the slough alongside.

Dogs: Canine companions should be on-leash when out of the boat and on the trail to Widgeon Falls. The hike is not busy on weekdays.

Of Interest: Metro Vancouver has recently passed over control of the launch point at Grant Narrows Regional Park to the Katzie First Nation. It will be exciting to see what plans they have for this area in the future.

Eco-Insight: Harbour Seals & Sea Lions

The harbour seal is a virtually guaranteed sight in ocean habitat surrounding Metro Vancouver, but Pitt Lake and the slough are fresh water – what's up? Let's look at the connections. Widgeon Slough connects to Pitt Lake, which in turn drains into the Pitt River. The Pitt River flows into the Fraser River, which finally connects with the Strait of Georgia in the Pacific Ocean, which is, of course, where marine mammals normally live. The harbour seals are following their source of food – salmon. Therefore, although it seems odd to see harbour seals in a lake, it makes sense, because this is where their food has led them.

Here is a little evolutionary history as it relates to this marine mammal. Harbour seals are earless (technically, they do have ears – just not external ear flaps), while sea lions are eared seals. Scientists believe that both were land mammals that took to the oceans about 20 million years ago, long after whales and dolphins did the same. Today we see harbour seals and sea lions as similar animals in a similar habitat, but it is thought that harbour seals evolved from an otter-like ancestor, while sea lions evolved from a very dissimilar bear-like mammal. Understanding evolutionary history helps make other connections, such as comprehending global distribution of species or how species adapted to changing environments.

Seals are very curious and will often watch or even follow along

ABOVE: *A marine mammal that you are likely to see on your paddle is the harbour seal.*

OPPOSITE TOP: *There is nothing quite like the pleasure of a beautiful day on the water.* (PHOTO COURTESY OF JILL SIMPSON)

OPPOSITE BOTTOM: *If you can, plan some of your activities around sharing the joy of nature with children.*

with you, so keep your eyes open for the glossy rounded head of this animal at the water's surface.

Other Area Interests

Extra time on this day can be spent at Pitt Polder dykes for a walk to the birding towers, or you can plan a trip to the Coquitlam watershed for one of their watershed tours that are run on several weekends during the summer.

Other Adventures

"Happiness is not a matter of intensity but of balance, order, rhythm, and harmony."

—Thomas Merton, *The Way of Chuang-Tzu*, 1965

Being a generalist in my recreational activities provides not just diversity in my life but balance as well. As much as I do one sport, any new activity seems to hint at new muscles I didn't know I had. To some, multiple activities means they are cross-training, while others see it as variety. Ultimately, I think, it's about balance in our lives – that elusive goal we are seeking in so many aspects of our world. Of course, balance isn't an illusion; it's completely within our control. For if it's not in our control, then in whose control is it? I ask that you see this chapter not just as an avenue to new recreational activities but also to new ideas and ways of approaching health and happiness. I ask that you connect it to encouraging yourself to step out of your comfort zone as you try something new. Finally, I ask that you consider recreation as a holistic way to achieve a balance in life that provides a strong foundation to build on for the other areas of your life, including work, relationships or community involvement.

According to the latest neuroscience research, learning new activities opens new neural pathways. Physical exercise stimulates multiple brain regions, improving brain function and protecting against cognitive decline. The human brain is able to continually adapt and rewire itself; brain development is not limited to childhood. Therefore, while struggling to become proficient at a new activity, think of this: your brain has plasticity and has the capacity to shape and reorganize itself according to new experiences. This body-mind interaction is what stimulates your brain cells to grow and connect with each other in complex ways. Therefore, as you paddle (or row, or run, or ride), know that as you do, branches of intricate nerve fibres called dendrites (Latin for "tree") are making new connections. These dendrites are the antennas through which neurons send and receive communication. You are not only working new muscles, you are improving the structural basis of your brain's memory capacity and thinking ability.

This chapter highlights a selection of further activities that should complement the other chapters of this book. They vary from something common to most – walking (on Salt Spring Island), to a sport still relatively new to Metro Vancouver – paddleboarding. One activity entices you to swim in a stunning Coquitlam lake, while another encourages you to attempt rowing sculls on Deas Slough in Ladner. Geographically, this chapter's activities lead you north to Whistler for a skate ski, and west to the Gulf Islands for a walk. Finally, the following pages guide you to what we sometimes think of as more extreme sports. These include mountain biking on the North Shore and rock climbing in Squamish, though extreme is *not* what they have to be for you to enjoy them. All of the recreational activities in this chapter, and in this book, can be practiced safely and as a means of fun and enjoyment. Our lives are flooded with images of sports taken to extreme ends, but the pursuits discussed in this book engage us on a spectrum. The extent to which you engage is up to you.

(PHOTO COURTESY OF VALERIE BELANGER)

Swimming at Sasamat Lake in Belcarra Park

Distance: 1 – 2 km
Time: 30 min. – 1 hr.
Level: easy – moderate
Public Transit Routes: 150, C26 "Port Moody/Belcarra" (see Notes)

Activity Highlight

In summer, this is probably the warmest lake in Metro Vancouver. It can be crazy busy during the day, but when the sun stops striking its beaches, it clears out quickly. Enter the swimmers! It's a decent length of a swim from White Pine Beach to the Sasamat Camp dock. The lake is calm, free of obstacles and mostly clear. If you enjoy outdoor swimming and desire a change from a winter of doing laps in a pool, then you will enjoy this activity.

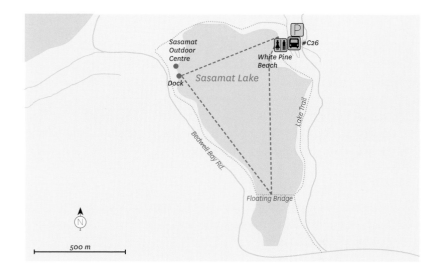

The evening light on a late summer's swim

(PHOTO COURTESY OF TREVOR BONAS)

Directions

From White Pine Beach, swim west to the dock at Sasamat Outdoor Centre. A return swim from the beach is approximately 1 km. A further swim is possible by swimming a triangle route: White Pine Beach to the outdoor centre dock (500 m), then southeast to the floating walkway (725 m), then northeast to White Pine Beach (650 m). This swim ends up being just under 2 km. This route allows you to stay close to the shore for most of the swim.

Notes

Transit & Transportation: The #150 is a summer-only bus. The c26 "Port Moody/Belcarra" runs all year and will get you close, but not right to the day use area.

Maps: You can find maps for the trails online at Metro Vancouver Parks (metrovancouver.org/services/parks_lscr/regionalparks/Pages/Belcarra.aspx), but there is no specific map for this swim. Use the map on this page as a guide.

Restrooms: These are available at White Pine Beach.

Safety: I suggest wearing a wetsuit for swimming in lakes as it acts as both a buoyancy device to keep you at the surface and a means of warmth. Wearing a bright-coloured swim cap ensures boats or other swimmers can see you easier too. In addition, I suggest to always swim with somebody – it's much more fun and safe that way. Finally, the lake also harbours a fair amount of geese. Watch for signage at the water's edge to see if Metro Vancouver Parks is concerned about the fecal coliform count in the lake – often associated with the geese.

Timing: This can be a very warm lake in mid – late August – sometimes it feels like a cool bathtub. My favourite time to swim in this lake is after the sunbathers have gone home (at about 6:30 pm when the sun is low in the summer sky). However, this means the sun can be in your eyes during the swim, so you may wish to have coloured goggles. Be aware that the park closes its gates at sunset and does not allow people on, or in, the lake after park hours.

Dogs: This activity is not suitable for dogs. Dogs are also not permitted on White Pine Beach.

Eco-Insight: The Value of Lakes

What is the value of a lake? No doubt, ethereal beauty comes to mind. Recreation, such as swimming in Sasamat, is certainly a value. If you filled your water bottle from a tap, then a lake's importance to our water supply may enter your thoughts. Do you fish recreationally? Then a stocked lake is sure to be of value to you. If you own a home on the edge of one, your property values are probably higher because of it. Larger lakes offer even more. They supply water to industry, support aquaculture and commercial fishing and provide transportation corridors. Do you see the connection between these? They all revolve around their value to *us*. However, we are not the only users; other life forms require them as well.

Lakes are critical stopover areas for migrating birds. Many waterfowl such as loons use them to breed, nest and raise their young. Kokanee salmon utilize BC interior lakes for spawning. Edges of lakes are critical habitat for insect larvae, which, in turn, are essential for sustaining fish populations. The flying insects over a lake are equally

The tree frog is a common species found near temperate forest lakes.
(PHOTO COURTESY OF ROB ALEXANDER)

Canada geese are common all year throughout Metro Vancouver, including here at Sasamat Lake. (PHOTO COURTESY OF TERRY BEREZAN)

valuable to bats and swallows. Interior lakes are important habitat for mammals such as moose, and essential ecosystems for amphibians such as frogs, newts and salamanders.

Swimming is a sport that allows me to think clearly. I consider challenges and issues in my life while face forward in the water. Perhaps while you swim, consider the state of lakes and water in British Columbia, Canada and the world. What do you know about them and how vital do you think this habitat is for a healthy future?

Other Area Interests: Noteworthy Swimming Sites

At 137 m in length, Kitsilano Pool ("Kits" pool) is Canada's longest outdoor pool (see the Stanley Park to Kits ride in the cycling chapter of this book) – almost three times longer than an Olympic pool – and Vancouver's only heated saltwater pool. This makes it a noteworthy and recommended swimming site. Another option is any one of Metro Vancouver's beaches. A favourite of mine is swimming off Crescent Beach in South Surrey.

Walking on Salt Spring Island

Distance: 12 – 15 km
Time: full day
Level: moderate
Grade: moderate < 95 m
Public Transit Routes: SkyTrain/Canada Line, 620 (see Notes), BC Ferries (Tsawwassen to Galiano, Mayne, Pender, Salt Spring and Saturna islands)

Activity Highlight

If you catch the right ferry that goes directly to Salt Spring, you can spend a fair amount of a day walking and exploring this Gulf Island treasure. We often have boundaries in our minds about how far we can go for a day trip, placing the Strait of Georgia Gulf Islands in our summer vacation category. If this resembles your thinking, then perhaps it's time to expand your boundaries. The Gulf Islands, including Salt Spring, are easy day trips, but with the logistical issue of a ferry. However, if you don't plan to take a vehicle, then the logistics get much simpler. Just arrive on time as a foot passenger and plan for the most direct ferry crossing. One day on Salt Spring and I promise you it will feel like you were just on vacation.

Directions

From the Tsawwassen Ferry Terminal, it is as simple as walking on the ferry and getting off at the Long Harbour dock on Salt Spring Island. Follow the Long Harbour Road (wait for the cars from the ferry to go by first) to Upper Ganges Road and then to Lower Ganges Road. Note that the ferry takes reservations – even for foot passengers! At the time of writing, the reservations are free and are necessary on busy days, such as weekends and holidays, during the summer.

Notes

Transit & Transportation: The #620 bus goes to the Tsawwassen Ferry Terminal. From there, you walk on and off the ferry. Note that the ferry

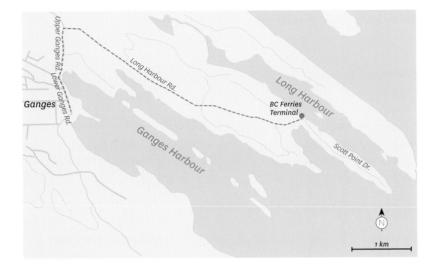

to Salt Spring Island can be long due to several stops at other Gulf Islands prior to Salt Spring. If you take a ferry that stops at all of the islands, then plan on a three-hour-plus ferry ride. There is a 1.5-hour, nonstop, Tsawwassen to Galiano, Mayne, Pender, Salt Spring and Saturna islands ferry (often provided on weekends and holidays). Salt Spring has a limited bus service on the island if you decide on staying late for dinner. Check into the Salt Spring Island Transit System and bus #4 to Long Harbour, but be aware the times may not always work due to the buses' early cut-off time.

Maps: You can find maps of the island on the ferry, or you can have them sent to you from Tourism BC (hellobc.com).

Restrooms: These are located at the ferry dock and in Ganges.

Safety: This activity does have you walking on a road with many blind corners. Be aware of traffic while walking.

Timing: Plan accordingly in the winter, as ferry times are more sporadic.

Company: This is a good place to take visitors in the summer to give them a feel for British Columbia's west coast.

Dogs: Furry friends should be on a leash as this walk is along a road from the ferry terminal to Ganges.

Although the ferry will determine your timing on Salt Spring Island, if you can be there around sunset, you will see the glow of the shoreline and arbutus.

Of Interest: Salt Spring Island is the largest of the Gulf Islands and has long been a very special place in British Columbia. There are large numbers of artists, sculptors and musicians living here, so if you have an interest in art and culture, then you may wish to plan your trip during one of the island's summer art festivals.

This walk is interesting as the environment is quite different from Metro Vancouver. Here, you are in the dry Douglas fir zone. Look for differences on your walk and compare it to other sites you may have covered in this book, such as Minnekhada Regional Park.

Eco-Insight: The Rain Shadow Effect

Coastal BC weather generally comes from the Pacific Ocean. West winds bring air masses characteristic of the regions where they were created – sometimes tropical, sometimes arctic. As an air mass from the west encounters the mountains of Vancouver Island, it rises, which causes it to cool (air cools at a temperature lapse rate of 6.5°C/1000 m). Often the water vapour condenses to droplets (the air's capacity to hold water vapour decreases as it cools), which fall to the ground, resulting in heavy precipitation on the western side of the island. With the water "squeezed" out of the air mass on the windward side, it continues its path down the leeward (eastern) side of the mountains, where the cooling effect is reversed as it falls – drier and warmer conditions are the result. This is the air that flows over the Gulf Islands, rendering them a dry zone. With less water and warmer weather, Gulf Islands such as Salt Spring look and feel very different from, say, Tofino.

The forest on Salt Spring is predominantly Douglas fir – different from the forests of Metro Vancouver or western Vancouver Island. Accompanying the Douglas fir are grand fir, arbutus, lodgepole pine, Garry oak and western yew – all of which are much rarer, or nonexistent, on the mainland. This sets up an ecosystem with a Mediterranean climate that supports a unique assemblage of plants, insects, amphibians and birds. It also positions this area to be home to many rare and endangered species that exist only in this narrow rain shadow band.

If you don't understand why British Columbia has many endangered species, this is a good place to learn more. Notice the development and forestry pressures. Listen to the conversations between

If you are on any Gulf Island in late summer, be sure to try the salal berries, and don't worry about the blue teeth you will get. It'll help you blend in with the locals.

islanders in the Ganges coffee shop. Read the bulletin board at the grocery store. You will begin to see that those living on the island place great value on this unique ecosystem.

Other Area Interests: Noteworthy Walking Sites

Many areas in Metro Vancouver are great places for walking. Other areas include Pacific Spirit Park and the University of British Columbia, the Burnaby Mountain trails around Simon Fraser University, the West Vancouver Seawall or any number of heritage walking tours (Chinatown, Yaletown, Gastown or Shaughnessy) offered throughout Metro Vancouver.

Rowing Sculls on Deas Slough in Ladner

Distance: 3 – 12 km
Time: 2 hrs.
Level: moderately difficult
Public Transit Route: 640

Activity Highlight

Do you like precision, technique and systems in the skills you develop? If yes, then I highly recommend rowing. It took me some time to warm up to the sport as the learning curve can be steep, but the payoff is great. As a beginner, you will be concentrating on left hand over right, catching the water, knees down, opening your back and then not racing up that slide, so the fact there's a heron feeding at the slough's edge may go unnoticed or become just another deadhead to be avoided. But as you improve, there will be plenty of opportunities to stop and watch the abundance of eagles in the trees that line the slough, overhead or swooping low over the water. It helped that the Delta Deas Rowing Club (deltadeas.com) has such friendly, welcoming people who supported me. They, and other Metro Vancouver rowing clubs, offer many opportunities to participate or just to try the sport out. Rowing is easy on the joints, a great full-body workout for your core, legs, arms and back and it connects you to a community. Rowing also provides serenity – there is a meditative aspect to it that few sports provide. Oh, and one more thing, due to the muscles used in the sport, rowers' butts look awesome!

Directions

Contact the Delta Deas Rowing Club on Deas Island about learn-to-row options. Make your way to Deas Island Regional Park. There is a big parking lot on your left as you enter the park and the rowing shed and dock are at the end of the parking lot. This location is at the head of Deas Slough. The slough is a protected body of water, perfect for rowing.

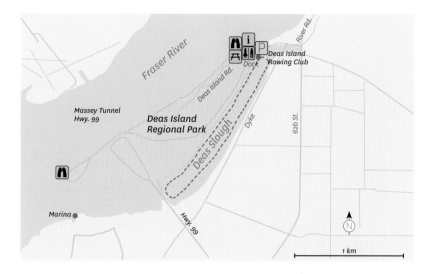

Notes

Maps: These are unnecessary, although you may wish to use the map on this page to understand the area and where the rowing takes place.

Restrooms: These are available at Deas Island Park. If you get yourself into a rowing quad and have to go – sorry, buddy, you're out of luck. Once you're on the water, you're there to row. *I've been there, done that.*

Safety: Bring extra clothes (to store on land) as you row on the water. You can trust your safety to the professional instructors and the powered safety boat provided by the club. You don't wear a life preserver when rowing (though they are with the coach boat); therefore, you should be a proficient swimmer.

Timing: April through September is the time the Delta Deas Rowing Club offers learn-to-row courses, though they row all year barring no ice on the slough In addition, they have days that volunteers invite the public to try out rowing.

Dogs: Canine companions are not appropriate with this sport.

Of Interest: Rowing is an inclusive sport and suitable for all ages (teens through to older adults) and abilities. Rowing itself isn't difficult, though I have labelled it a moderately difficult sport due to the time it takes to become proficient enough to row in a stable manner.

ABOVE: *A sport with beautiful geometry* (PHOTO COURTESY OF STUART MCCALL)
OPPOSITE: *The varnish clam is an invasive species, only first seen in BC in the early 1980s. Today it is one of the more common clams to find on the southwest coast of BC.* (PHOTO COURTESY OF ROB ALEXANDER)

Eco-Insight: Invasive Species

Can you name three invasive species in Metro Vancouver? Unless invasive species directly affect you, you may find this difficult. If our local native species had voices, however, answering this question would be easy. Many Metro Vancouver habitats have invasive species, but those frequented by people and bordering water are the most vulnerable areas. An invasive species is a non-native organism that has negative effects on our economy, natural heritage, environment or our health. The most aggressive species are those that reproduce rapidly and cause major changes to the areas where they become established. They are a major threat to biodiversity in Metro Vancouver and globally.

Here are a few invasive plant species that local organizations are trying to prevent from gaining a foothold, to eradicate or to control: Japanese knotweed, purple loosestrife, kudzu, giant hogweed, Eurasian water milfoil, Scotch broom and English ivy. Other invasive organisms found in Metro Vancouver are the American bullfrog, common carp, yellow perch, eastern grey squirrel and zebra mussel.

Would you like to know more? Before you head to the slough, check out the Invasive Species Council of Metro Vancouver (iscmv.ca) for profiles on invasive species, target areas, containment areas and invasive-free zones. You can make a lasting difference in your community if you get to know invasive species. There are always volunteer opportunities to help with plant pulls, to collect information and to educate others.

Other Area Interests: Noteworthy Rowing Sites

There are many clubs to join and places to row in Metro Vancouver, including Deep Cove, Burnaby Lake, Surrey (at Nicomekl River), Vancouver (Stanley Park) and False Creek.

Rowing is truly a community sport, always done with a coach boat and often with fellow rowers in a quad or double.

(PHOTO COURTESY OF STUART MCCALL)

Inline Skating at the Lower Seymour Conservation Reserve

Distance: 18 km
Time: 1.5 – 3 hrs.
Level: difficult (see Notes)
Grade: difficult < 275 m
Public Transit Route: 228 (see Notes)

Activity Highlight

If you already have strong inline skating skills and can manage hills, turns and speed, then you will enjoy this activity. If your skills are rustier, then check out the Other Area Interests listed below for easier skating. Inline skating is fun, fast and a great workout. Nevertheless, if you push beyond your skills, it can also be quite dangerous. The Seymour Valley offers an auto-free experience as it meanders through temperate forest. However, North Shore forests are not flat, and neither is this trail. It undulates its way 9 km into the delightful Seymour Valley watershed.

Directions

Take Exit 22A off Highway 1 for Capilano University and continue 5 km north on Lillooet Road to the Rice Lake Gate parking area. In the reserve, follow the Seymour Valley Pathway to the 9-km mark.

Notes

Transit & Transportation: Bus #228 goes to the edge of the Seymour Valley. From the corner of Dempsey and Lynn Valley Road, you will have to walk 500 m to the start at Rice Lake Gate.

Maps: You can find maps for the trails online at Metro Vancouver Parks (metrovancouver.org/services/parks_lscr/regionalparks) or at Rice Lake Gate. Ask for the Lower Seymour Conservation Reserve (LSCR) map.

Restrooms: These are located at the Rice Lake Gate and at various points on the Seymour Pathway.

Safety: When inline skating, wear a proper-fitting helmet and padding

for your elbows, hands and knees. Take off your inline skates and walk down hills if you think you will not be in control. Use a map and be sure to plan for enough daylight hours. Remember the pathway is slippery when it's wet or when it has fall leaves on it.

Timing: The Seymour Valley Pathway should be dry; therefore, summer is the best time for this activity.

Dogs: No dogs are permitted north of the Rice Lake Gate.

Of Interest: You can rent inline skates from local businesses in North Vancouver.

Eco-Insight: Historic Logging on the North Shore

This activity takes you nine kilometres into the Seymour Valley. The upper valley (above the dam) is the watershed for a large percentage of Metro Vancouver's water. In addition to water, the Seymour Valley also has an important history of logging. Look at the forest around you. It is mainly composed of Douglas fir, western hemlock, western red cedar, red alder, bigleaf maple and black cottonwood. Now look at the height of the trees. How old do you think this forest might be? Here is a hint: the trees are only a fraction of the height of those that existed here until the 19th century. In fact, the skyline of this area was, on average, higher than the skyline of downtown Vancouver today!

The LSCR paved pathway leads 9 km into the Seymour Valley and through a lush temperate forest of cedar, fir and hemlock. This undulating pathway has hills that should only be attempted by proficient in-line skaters.

During the height of logging in the first three decades of the 1900s, this area was home to springboards, crosscut saws, steam donkeys, flume lines, skid or corduroy logging roads and loggers to run them all. In the early days, red cedar was the most desirable commercial tree. Dynamite was used to split the especially large trees – those that had been around for millennia or more. You will notice lining this pathway are cedar stumps containing notches used to support springboards, platforms on which loggers stood to raise themselves above the extra-wide tree trunks at the base, making cutting down the trees that much easier. The felled trees were pulled through the forest by steam donkeys (steam-powered winches) or bucked up into manageable lengths and floated down flume lines (wooden troughs filled with water). Next, they were loaded onto carts pulled by horses and oxen along skid or corduroy roads built from logs placed side to side, perpendicular to the direction of the road, creating a more solid, but still bumpy, surface through the mossy terrain. Finally, the cedar lengths were split into shakes and shingles for early Vancouver homes. By the

The reconstructed flume line on the path to Rice Lake was essentially a waterslide for wood cuts called shinglebolts. Early 20th century logging supplied BC mills that made shakes and shingles for Vancouver's growing population. (PHOTO COURTESY OF ROB ALEXANDER)

early 20th century, most of the big cedar was gone and loggers moved on to Douglas fir for its straight and strong lumber. No logging exists anymore on the North Shore, although some trees are still being removed for forest fire management.

Your home probably has fir beams in its frame, while your roof may have cedar shingles. On the coast, foresters cut hemlock for pulp and paper, spruce and fir for lumber and plywood and a myriad of other products we use.

Other Area Interests: Noteworthy Inline Skating Sites

The following paved trail sites are more suitable for beginners than the Seymour Valley Pathway: PoCo trail from the Red Bridge to Lions Park, Stanley Park Seawall (or any seawall in the centre part of Vancouver), the North Shore Spirit Trail, the Vancouver-Burnaby Central Valley Greenway (between Renfrew and Douglas), the New Westminster Quay to the BC Parkway and the Burnaby Mountain Urban Trail.

Stand-Up Paddleboarding in Deep Cove

Distance: 1 – 3 km
Time: 1 – 2 hrs.
Level: moderate
Public Transit Routes: 211, 212, C15

Activity Highlight

Is one of your goals this year to learn a new sport? This may be the one. Paddleboarding is a relatively new sport born out of Hawaii that bears some resemblance to surfing but with a paddle. It is becoming increasingly popular on the West Coast and there are multiple places to rent the equipment. Deep Cove is one of those places and offers a protected area and lessons to learn this sport. Expect a change of perspective from a kayak or canoe as you look out across the water from an elevation. At this level, you see into the water much better than in a kayak so it is easier to see jellies and other species in the shallow water. Finally, expect to use new muscles in your body, including your core.

Directions

Rent your paddleboard from Deep Cove Canoe & Kayak (deepcove kayak.com) and launch from there. Note that Deep Cove can be busy launching many of its own boats, so be aware that this is a potentially busy area. Reservations are recommended on weekends, or anytime in July and August.

Notes

Maps: These are not necessary for this activity if you plan to stay in and around the cove.

Restrooms: These are available next to the rental shop at Deep Cove Canoe & Kayak.

Safety: Never leave your board; if you lose the paddle, you can paddle it with your hands. Stay attached to your board with an ankle leash while in, sorry, I mean *on* the ocean.

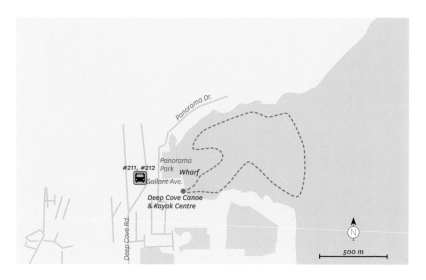

Dogs: Many people take dogs paddleboarding and Deep Cove Canoe & Kayak doesn't discourage it. In fact, it even offers a "S'up Dawg" event!

Of Interest: This is a relatively new sport to Vancouver and most people rent their paddleboards rather than have their own. Therefore, the rental locations are closely associated with the areas you are most likely to see other stand-up paddleboarders.

Most rental locations have lessons as well as rentals. If you have never paddleboarded, consider a lesson. Watch for specials, such as a free introductory day, to try out a paddleboard at no charge (Deep Cove Canoe & Kayak [deepcovekayak.com] has offered these in the past).

Eco-Insight: Habitat Restoration

People have the capacity to alter habitat for better or worse. The news often focuses on the bad and we begin to believe that little good is happening. However, much good in habitat restoration *is* happening, and it stems from governments, clubs and organizations, for-profits and nonprofits, kindergarten classes and university programs. It is just that habitat restoration often doesn't have the same ability to grab headlines as environmental degradation does. Let's consider what good in habitat restoration is happening in Metro Vancouver.

Volunteering for an ivy pull at Stanley Park (PHOTO COURTESY OF DON ENRIGHT)

Streamside plantings by Scouts and Guides reduce erosion and provide shade to salmon fry. Ivy and other invasive plant removals by volunteers at Stanley Park Ecology Society create space for planting native bushes such as salmonberry and salal. Eelgrass is being planted at low tide by the Squamish River Watershed Society to encourage herring to spawn again as they did in the past. Homeowners are "greenscaping" their properties by encouraging native plants, stopping the use of pesticides and setting up birdhouses. Schools are portioning parts of their landscape for growing plants and teaching outdoors. You don't have to look far beyond any Metro Vancouver neighbourhood to find examples of habitat restoration, nor do you have to look far for the leadership that ensures it takes place.

The wider connection, of course, is that humans deeply affect the environment in a myriad of ways, and wild species usually face the brunt of this impact. However, we also have amazing capacity and vision to have a positive influence on environments around us – and we do! Have a look around to see what good is happening in your neighbourhood.

What better way to begin a day than with an early morning stand-up paddleboard workout in Deep Cove. (PHOTO COURTESY OF VIVIANE NISHIKIORI)

Other Area Interests: Noteworthy Stand-Up Paddleboarding Sites

You can also rent paddleboards from White Rock beach or from Ecomarine Paddlesport Centres at Granville Island, English Bay or the Sailing Centre at Jericho Beach.

Mountain Biking on the North Shore

Distance: 5 – 10 km
Time: 2 – 3 hrs.
Level: moderate
Public Transit Route: 228 (see Notes)

Activity Highlight

Many trails are available on the North Shore for mountain biking, however, few are for the beginner rider. This activity aims to appeal to those wanting to enter, or try out, the sport. The Richard Juryn Trails in the Seymour Valley are easy to access, close to bike rental shops and balance the right amount of challenging single track with ease of learning. You won't be bored, nor should you go home sore and scraped. There is a large and passionate mountain biking community on the North Shore and the trails are well established and maintained. Expect to get hooked, not by a cedar branch but by the mountain biking bug, as you wind your way through the undulating forest trails.

Directions

There are two great introductory trails that are mostly undulating, cross-country, single-track trails and among the best the North Shore offers for beginner riding. Rent a bike (see Rentals/Tips below) in North Vancouver and then get yourself to Lynn Creek at the Upper Levels Highway near the Park and Tilford Shopping Centre. Take the trail behind Mountain Equipment Co-op through Inter River Park and onto the road toward the Lower Seymour Conservation Reserve.

If you have a car, follow the road north up Lillooet Road from the Second Narrows Bridge and drive past the cemetery a few kilometres to the end of the road. Parking is near the Rice Lake Gate. Follow the paved pathway to the first picnic area across from Rice Lake to find the Circuit 8 Trail Loop. The majority of these trails are flat and are well suited for every level of rider looking to hone their bike skills. Ride up the path on the right side of the road for 400 m and then turn right along the Richard Juryn Trails. This second trail is also north of the

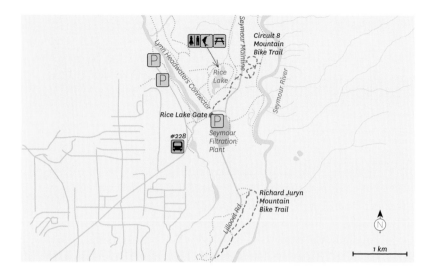

Rice Lake Gate. Ride both trails each way, as they will feel like a completely different trail in the opposite direction. Expect to be in this area for 2 – 3 hours if you aim to complete both rides in multiple directions.

Notes

Transit & Transportation: Bus #228 goes to the edge of the Seymour Valley. From Dempsey and Lynn Valley Road, ride 500 m to the start at Rice Lake Gate.

Maps: The Lower Seymour Conservation Reserve has a good map, as do many local North Shore bike shops. The shops have more detailed books and maps on many of the local trails. Their resources offer more thorough directions, more options and more background on the trails than is offered in this book. Finally, the North Shore Trail Map available at Mountain Equipment Co-op covers this and many other trail areas on the North Shore and is an invaluable map if you plan to spend time in this area.

Restrooms: These are located near Rice Lake Gate and along the Seymour Pathway.

Safety: Well-fitting gear, including helmet, pads, gloves, protective glasses and armour, is essential. Bring a basic first aid kit for small cuts

Do you know a teen you would like to join you on an activity? Mountain biking on the North Shore may be a good option.

and bumps. Understand how the bike works. Understand the rules of the trail, as there are likely to be others behind and in front of you.

Timing: Spring can be mucky, so summer and early fall are the best times for mountain biking on the North Shore. The North Shore has a diversity of trails, though many are intermediate to difficult. I suggest speaking to people at local bike shops in the community you intend to ride to get the best and latest trail information. Sometimes trails close for maintenance or upgrades.

Company: Do you know a teenager who likes mountain biking? Get a teen to join you on this activity and, possibly, even be your guide!

Dogs: Canine companions are not appropriate for this activity.

Rentals/Tips: Endless Biking (endlessbiking.com) in North Vancouver is a full-service mountain bike business. It rents bikes and safety gear packages for approximately \$55 – \$95 for four hours (as of 2014). In addition, it offers tours, lessons and shuttle services. You can also easily ride from the rental shop to the trails mentioned above.

Eco-Insight: Soil

Be careful…It's entirely possible that mountain biking may lead to a mouthful of dirt! Soil surrounds you in this activity. It won't be just on your tires and bike frame but also on your shoes, pants and hands, and possibly on your helmet and face. Dirt just goes with the sport. So let's have a closer look at what makes up soil.

While biking in this temperate forest, try this: choose an area the size of your hand and scrape the top, duff layer (leaves and needles) aside, exposing the dark, coffee-coloured soil below. Now place about a teaspoon of soil in the palm of your hand. Believe it or not, you are holding approximately one billion single-celled organisms, comprised of about 4,000 different species (mostly bacteria), and almost all of these are completely unknown to science! Though a few of the organisms are reproducing, most of them are dormant. They are waiting for the right combination of moisture, temperature and nutrients to which they are adapted before continuing their life cycle. The biological activity going on beneath your wheels is a complex underground ecosystem of microbes, earthworms, mites, insects and fungi, and the health of the shrubs, ferns and trees here depends on it. Soil is the foundation upon which the rest of terrestrial life depends, yet even scientists know only a small portion of what this microbial world has to offer.

Other Area Interests: Noteworthy Mountain Biking Sites

There are many famous trails in the North Shore, but they are mostly for intermediate to advanced riders. For beginner riding, consider areas on Burnaby Mountain, Green Timbers in Surrey or Pacific Spirit Park near the University of British Columbia.

Go Further: Skate/Classic Cross-Country Skiing in Whistler's Callaghan Valley

Distance: 5 – 20 km
Time: 1 – 4 hrs.
Level: easy – moderate
Grade: moderate < 75 m
Public Transit Routes: no transit

Activity Highlight

One legacy of the 2010 Olympics is the access to the Callaghan Valley and the diversity of ski trails within it. Ski Callaghan (skicallaghan.ca) is the union of Callaghan Country and the Whistler Olympic Park. Between their combined facilities, this area is the largest cross-country ski area in North America! While classic skiing is familiar to most Canadians, skate skiing is still catching on. Classic skiing allows you to pause and take in the winter world, whereas a pause with skate skiing just has you drawing in more oxygen! Both have their place and once you get the weight transfer down for either, they are wonderful sports to enjoy. In addition, they are full-body workouts that are easy on your joints. Callaghan Valley was world class for the Olympics and it is world class now. If you haven't checked it out yet, then now is the time.

Directions

Take Highway 99 (Sea-to-Sky Highway) about 30 minutes past Squamish and watch for a blue "Recreation Area" sign with icons for cross-country skiing and other sports. This is the Callaghan Valley Access Road. Turn left and drive 8.5 – 9 km to the Ski Callaghan ticketing area.

Notes

Maps: These are located at the ticket areas. Ski Callaghan offers about 130 km of groomed track-set ski trails.

Restrooms: These are located near the day lodges.

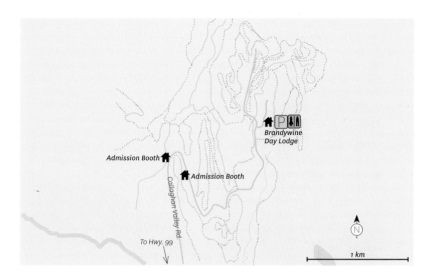

Safety: The trails at Callaghan are long. Treat this activity as if you're heading into the backcountry and let someone know where you will be skiing and what time you will be returning. Wear a backpack containing food and drink, extra clothing and a basic first aid kit.

Timing: Skiing in the Callaghan Valley often begins in late November and ends in early April.

Dogs: Ski with your pooch – many of Ski Callaghan's trails are dog-friendly and it's easy to do a nice 10-km loop with a dog. Note that all dogs are required to display a Ski Callaghan pet pass while on the trails.

Of Interest: On Wednesdays there is five kilometres of night-lit trails. This area also offers many snowshoe trails with a trail pass.

Rentals/Tips: Ski rentals are available at Callaghan Country and at Whistler Olympic Park.

Eco-Insight: Wintering Birds in British Columbia

What do birds do in the fall? They migrate, right? Well not all species do. In fact, some stick it out in British Columbia for the long winter months, just like most of the local people do. Coastal British Columbia is also warm enough to attract and retain migrating winter birds from more northerly climes, such as raptors, swans and geese.

ABOVE: *Skate skiing with Solitude glacier in the background.* (PHOTO
COURTESY OF BRAD SILLS)

OPPOSITE: *Birds adapt to winter. We may expect to see the chickadee
all year round, but it is always a surprise to see a very tropical looking
Anna's hummingbird still around when snow arrives.*

These congregate around the mild waters of Metro Vancouver's sea-shores, lakes and sloughs. When you leave the coast and move inland, the temperature cools but still you will find birds that don't migrate at all. These residents, such as the examples listed below, embrace winter, adapting to its chill. While on the trails around Whistler, watch closely for these adaptable birds that provide a delightful insight into the natural world if you pay attention. Here are a few to watch for.

- *Chickadees* – These birds survive freezing nights by huddling together and going into a state called torpor. This short-term hibernation state slows body functions (heart rate, respiration and metabolism), allowing the birds to conserve energy and heat.

- *Grey jays (whiskey jacks)* – After accepting handouts from skiers, whiskey jacks will fly away, roll and bind the food in saliva, store it in conifers for later, then, in short order, come back for more.

- *Ravens* – These are among the cleverest of birds in Canada. They survive, in part, by having an incredibly varied diet of seeds, grains, insects, frogs, eggs, young birds and carrion.

- *Clark's nutcracker* – After collecting seeds in the summer months, these birds store them for winter. Over the winter, they will find and consume up to 70 per cent of the 100,000 (or so) seeds they stored in summer.

- *Ptarmigan* – Seasonally, these birds change colour to blend in with their surroundings and they grow more feathers on their feet (think snowshoes) to walk more efficiently on snow.

Other Area Interests: Noteworthy Cross-Country & Skate Skiing Sites

Strawberry Flats at Manning Park, the Cypress Bowl cross-country ski area and the Lost Lake cross-country ski area at Whistler are also great places near Metro Vancouver for these sports.

Go Further: Rock Climbing & Bouldering in Squamish

Time: full day
Level: moderate
Public Transit Routes: no transit

Activity Highlight

Have you been curious about the sport of rock climbing? Rock climbing is a fantastic workout that builds muscle and, if planned properly, is a safe and fun sport to add to your repertoire. It is different from other activities described in this book because it involves hiring a guide for a lesson. I chose to profile a guided introduction to the sport rather than describe a climb that requires existing rock climbing skills because there are still many people who have yet to attempt this sport in earnest. In fact, people come from around the planet to rock climb at the bluffs in Squamish, so I thought there was no better approach than to "climb" directly into this unique community with this activity.

An "Introduction to Rock Climbing" course means you can try the sport with little investment while learning some basic skills, such as cliff safety, equipment use and care, basic knots, belay skills, climbing technique and rappelling. No previous experience is necessary and Squamish Rock Guides (squamishrockguides.com) provides the equipment. Bouldering is a similar activity, but closer to the ground, that Squamish Rock Guides provides instruction in as well.

Directions

After registering for a half-day or a full day activity with Squamish Rock Guides, drive to the Squamish Starbucks (across from the McDonald's) to meet your guide on the appropriate course day.

Notes

Maps: These are not necessary for this activity, however, if this becomes your "new thing," there are several books dedicated to the climbing routes in and around Squamish.

There are several rock climbing programs for children to choose from in Squamish too. (PHOTO COURTESY OF JEN REILLY)

Restrooms: These are available at several climbing locations in Squamish.

Safety: Squamish Rock Guides are Association of Canadian Mountain Guide (ACMG) professional instructors. They begin teaching slowly by building trust and assessing the skill level of their clients. They provide the methodical, repetitious and step-by-step instruction to ensure clients learn the correct rules and systems in the right order. This builds a solid foundation for a long and safe climbing future.

Timing: Squamish Rock Guides do courses from March to September.

Dogs: Canine companions are not appropriate for this activity.

Of Interest: Rock climbing routes are rated by grade and pitch. Search for the Tick List on the Squamish Rock Guides website to see photos and variations of Squamish climbing routes. You may begin to notice

Learning to climb in Squamish (PHOTO COURTESY OF COLIN MOORHEAD)

the differences between the difficulty and danger levels of a 5.7 versus a 5.9 or a 5.11d climb. Climbing is technical and it takes commitment to fully learn the safety procedures. Learning requires instruction, not just on climbing but also on cliff safety, equipment use and care, basic knots, belay skills, proper climbing technique and rappelling.

Eco-Insight: Mushroom Harvesting

What's the connection between rock climbing and mushroom harvesting, you ask? Honestly, I can't see one. However, after years of teaching students in Squamish, I can't deny there's an overlap between students who love to climb and those fascinated by spending their downtime scouring the forest for "shrooms." Clearly, climbers are among those who love the outdoors, and the wider community of outdoor

Mushrooms that taste great (PHOTO COURTESY OF CHRISTINE GAIO)

enthusiasts are more apt to have an interest in wild harvesting. So for all you climbers *and* outdoor aficionados, this is for you.

Mushrooms are the "fruit" of fungus that live below the forest floor. The root-like structures from a mushroom are mycelium and these often are associated with the roots of a living tree. If you choose to harvest mushrooms, bear in mind it's important not to damage the mycelium when harvesting. *Break the mushroom only at the surface – no deeper.* When searching for mushrooms in southwestern British Columbia's forests, understand the connection between mushrooms, tree types and tree ages and the soil layer. To learn more about this connection, see Eco-Insight: Mycorrhizal Connections (page 76). Three species are particularly popular.

- *Pine mushrooms* – Found under conifers in coarse-textured soils. They will often be around huckleberries.

- *Morels* – Found in coniferous and hardwood forests and in gardens with bark mulch. They are most abundant in areas the year after a forest fire.

- *Chanterelles* – Found in old-growth conifer forests with a rich soil humus layer. Watch for them under forest litter.

Use proper harvesting techniques when gathering mushrooms. Learn what each looks like if you plan to develop this ancient skill. Pick, or cut, mushrooms singly. Don't disturb the forest floor, moss layers or the mycelia under it. Take only what you can eat.

Other Area Interests: Noteworthy Rock Climbing Sites

If you would rather begin your climbing career indoors, there are many gyms in Metro Vancouver to choose from. One of the larger businesses is Cliffhanger Indoor Rock Climbing (cliffhangerclimbing. com/). It has climbing routes for many levels and an array of introductory courses as well. If, on the other hand, you have some rock climbing skills already and own your equipment, then Juniper Point at Lighthouse Park is a good choice for a local climb. There are many cracks and features at the site and most routes are top roped with good bolts accessible from the top for setting up.

Active Picnic Adventures

*"With good friends…and good food on the board…we may well ask;
When shall we live if not now?"*

M.F.K. Fisher, *The Art of Eating*, 1954

The idea to include picnicking in this book came while I was researching and writing. So many locations were conducive not only to actively recreating but also stopping, contemplating and sharing the beauty of the site. Your perspective changes depending on the time you give to a landscape. I suspect you know what I mean. Driving allows you to see, and appreciate, a broad viewscape. Cycling slows you down, presents you with the hills you wouldn't have noticed in the car and focuses your awareness on the immediate. Running reduces the speed again, providing immediate feedback on the soles of your feet, knees and hips. Walking slows the pace to a more reflective understanding of a landscape, allowing completely new entries into your field of view – a dew-covered spider web, an owl in a tree, the song of a wren and the aroma of wild roses in bloom. The ultimate pleasure is a complete stop in the right location, allowing the environment to move around you rather than the other way around. This is where the picnic idea for this book was born. The theme of the book, however, is about being active, so the sites chosen require some, but not a lot of, effort.

In my view, picnics, like a nice dinner out, break up the routine of eating. They can be romantic, a way to bring a family closer or a place to have important conversations. With the right timing, weather, menu and the right company, of course, your picnic stop will be memorable. Good planning of a picnic will create an unforgettable experience for visitors. Planning and assembling a meal outdoors slows us down to think more deeply about the food we consume. This chapter suggests menu items and locations, along with directions and highlights for each. Remember to pack out everything you pack in and *leave no trace* that you were ever there. A good place to begin this chapter is with an Eco-Insight on the food you'll be packing.

In the previous sections of the book, I have recommended an array of other picnic sites. To summarize, they include:

- Jug Island at Belcarra by hike or kayak;

- Point Roberts at Lily Point;

- Seymour River at the 10-km mark on the pathway;

- High Knoll viewpoint at Minnekhada Park;

- Bowen Lookout or Dog Mountain Lookout on a winter snowshoe;

- East Beach Trail to Starboat Cove at Lighthouse Park;

- Dinky Peak at Mount Seymour.

Eco-Insight: Picnics & Pollination

Once you have filled your picnic basket, have a look to determine what items came to you via pollination. Did you bring fruit or vegetables? Something with nuts in it? How about beans? Do you have a spread derived from, say, chickpeas? Coffee? Chocolate? Juice? Soy? You get the idea. Pollination is required to produce much of what we eat. Estimates suggest 35 per cent of all global food production comes from crops dependent on pollinators. Bees may be the most well-known pollinators, but vertebrates such as bats and hummingbirds, and insects such as

Some of the many ways of pollination. What is in your picnic basket that needed pollination? (PHOTOS 2, 3 AND 4 COURTESY OF ROB ALEXANDER)

beetles and mosquitoes (yes, there is a use for them) do important pollination work too. Some do it by day (butterflies), while others do it at night (moths). The health of our pollinators is extremely important and it's not an understatement to say that declines in pollinator populations could lead to a significant threat to the integrity of global biodiversity, food webs and human health. Ultimately, the best insurance for pollination services is an abundance and diversity of pollinators. The greater the number and types of interactions that exist in an ecosystem, the more resilient that ecosystem is. Resilience is more important than ever with our changing climate.

Think of pollination as a free ecological service. Like photosynthesis or nutrient cycling, it happens in the background and we rarely consider how our survival depends on it. It is imperative that we understand the connection between the conservation and preservation of our natural ecosystems and the full range of life-support services they provide. Oh, by the way, are you wearing cotton? Yeah, that's been pollinated too!

Planning a picnic is half the fun. One suggestion is to visit your local farmers market on the way to your destination and choose among the products offered there. If packing food along a trail, consider portability, ease of serving, share-ability and whether it will keep. Also consider seasonal flavours when planning. These may include asparagus in May, cherries or strawberries in June, blueberries in July, nectarines and sweet corn in August, apples and pears in September and chocolate fondue with your campstove in the January snow.

There are plenty of quick food ideas for picnics. Spend some time in the local supermarket deli and be open to new foods. You can also find inspiration online, in recipe books or just by looking in your fridge. Here are a few ideas:

Shopping List Suggestions

- coleslaw, potato or pasta salad;
- watermelon, grapes or fruit salad;
- French baguette, cheese and cold cuts;
- lemonade, sparkling apple juice or a flask;
- tortillas with guacamole and salsa;
- supermarket deli foods such as crackers, pesto, tapenade, bruschetta, olives, goat cheese and brie, or, on a different note, a lumberjack (full-on meat) sandwich from Safeway works with many teenagers (!);
- world foods such as hummus, falafel, baba ghanoush, tabbouleh, naan bread and sushi.

Simple Recipes

- *Sandwich roll-ups:* tortillas filled with ingredients like cream cheese, spinach, hummus, shredded carrot, cabbage, cold cuts or avocado.
- *Caprese salad:* sliced vine-ripe tomatoes, fresh mozzarella, quality olive oil, leaves of fresh basil, salt and pepper.

- *Easy tacos:* soft shells, salsa, pinto beans, avocado, shredded cheddar and lettuce.

- *Summer lemonade:* watermelon and strawberry with lemon juice, sugar and water.

- *Desserts:* two-bite brownies, ready-made chocolate-dipped strawberries, banana bread or a favourite from a local bakery.

There is more to a picnic than just the food! Consider how you will eat it and what you will do after you eat. Here are a few additional tips:

- consider packing reusable plates, cups, containers and utensils instead of disposable ones;

- pack a blanket, basket, pannier or backpack to help carry your food and drink;

- don't forget napkins, a serrated knife, dish towel, trash bag, hand sanitizer, sunscreen and nontoxic insect repellant;

- bring along activity gear such as a frisbee, hacky sack, Nerf football or musical instruments.

Picnic Date

A big part of romance is location; contemplate the following:

- consider a nighttime or winter picnic rather than just a daytime or summer one;

- pick up a special dish from a favourite restaurant you both like;

- choose a blanket over a picnic table, and choose candles (pending no fire ban and *not* on the blanket!);

- plan some sort of surprise that is appropriate and relevant to both of you;

- remember wind, wasps, sand fleas, weather changes and rude people can all influence your picnic, so be aware of these and your ability to "go with the flow";

- finally, good tasty food is a must (i.e., hearty peasant loaf over a kaiser bun, gruyere over cheddar, spinach over lettuce, smoked salmon over canned salmon) – you get the idea!

LEFT: *Careful when picnicking to keep your food items close at hand, or you may be inadvertently sharing them with wildlife.*
(PHOTO COURTESY OF RORRI MCBLANE)

BELOW: *This is the company you want to keep while picnicking, those that bring their own food!*
(PHOTO COURTESY OF ROB ALEXANDER)

Admiralty Point in Belcarra Regional Park

Distance: 3 km
Time: 1 hr.
Level: easy
Grade: easy < 25 m
Public Transit Routes: 150, C25, C26 Port Moody/Belcarra (see Notes)
Surface: dirt

Activity Highlight

The walk to Admiralty Point provides great views of Indian Arm and Burrard Inlet from several rocky outcrops. The walk also offers beach areas with spots to swim, to sun yourself or to play with a dog at the water's edge. The area isn't terribly busy and you can often find a private area on a rocky outcrop to open a picnic basket and share a meal. Consider this location if you have visitors in town and want to show off a beautiful spot. Belcarra Park has been a picnicking area for many decades. If you wish to expand your picnicking, say, to 100 of your closest friends, you can do it here (on the grass field) with reservable shelters and electric barbecues too.

Directions

From the Belcarra parking area at the end of Tum Tumay Whueton Drive, take the trail south from the restroom building. Admiralty Point is a side trail to the right about 1.4 km from the start. The trail meanders through lush forests, around rocky outcrops and next to pocket beaches. You can also continue an extra half kilometre to a white shell beach, one of the parks archaeological middens.

Notes

Transit & Transportation: The #150 is a summer-only bus. The C25 and C26 Port Moody/Belcarra can be used all year.

Restrooms: These are available at the start of the trail.

TOP: *The start of this activity begins on the Barnston Island ferry.*
(PHOTO COURTESY OF CHRISTINE GAIO)

BOTTOM: *Consider bannock as an option for a picnic.*

Moms and tots out for a hike at Admiralty Point

(PHOTO COURTESY OF SHELLEY FRICK)

Dogs: Rover should be on-leash while on the trail.

Of Interest: Belcarra Park also has both saltwater and freshwater fishing, crabbing and scuba diving around offshore reefs and shipwrecks.

Barnston Island on the Fraser River

Distance: 3.5 – 10 km
Time: 20 min. – 1 hr.
Level: easy
Grade: easy 0 m
Public Transit Routes: no transit
Surface: paved

Activity Highlight

This picnic is a throwback to a simpler and more rural time. With the access by ferry, the old farmhouses and the odd dog that follows you around the island, this picnic provides a unique perspective on the region. Do you know any moderately active older adults that would enjoy this walk and have stories to tell of growing up in this area? If so, don't miss a chance to invite them to your picnic.

Directions

You can access this island via a free, five-minute ride on a cable ferry that is located at the eastern end of 104th Avenue in Surrey. You can get to the picnic area by going left (west) from the ferry and be there in 1.75 km, or you can cycle around the island for a total of 10 km for a more active outing.

Notes

Restrooms: These are available near the picnic tables at the extreme western end of the island.

Dogs: Canine companions on-leash are permitted on this island and although they are allowed off-leash while on the road, they must be under control at all times. An experience many years ago with my dog (who was not under control) saw her run off the road and into an outdoor horse paddock. She spooked the animals, putting her, and the horses, in danger.

Kanaka Creek in Maple Ridge

Distance: 1 – 3 km
Time: 15 – 45 min.
Level: easy
Grade: easy < 25 m
Public Transit Routes: 701, C49 (see Notes)
Surface: riverbed

Activity Highlight

The unique part of this picnic is not just the beauty of the falls, the rushing water and the forest glade that surrounds you, but if you look closely, there are plant fossils in the riverbed rocks. Remember, though, it is illegal to remove fossils from a Metro Vancouver regional park.

Directions

Begin at the parking area at the corner of 251st Street and 116th Avenue in Maple Ridge. Take the trail to Cliff Falls, cross the bridge and scamper down into the riverbed (in the mid to late summer the water should be low). I suggest following Kanaka Creek away from the falls to a spot that suits you. Note that trails surround the creek above.

Notes

Transit & Transportation: C49 only runs every two hours, so plan accordingly.

Restrooms: These are available at the entrance to the park.

Dogs: Canine companions are to be on-leash at all times in this park.

TOP: *Watch for birds such as the spotted towhee enjoying their own pic-nic near you.* (PHOTO COURTESY OF ROB ALEXANDER)

BOTTOM: *Building a forest shelter with children while summer picnicking*
(PHOTO COURTESY OF SHELLEY FRICK)

Derby Reach Regional Park in Langley

Distance: 2 km
Time: 5 min. – 1.5 hrs.
Level: easy
Grade: easy < 25 m
Public Transit Routes: 595, C62 (see Notes)
Surface: gravel

Activity Highlight

The beauty of this park is its location on the working end of the Fraser River. This picnic will introduce you to one of the few urban camping spots in Metro Vancouver, as well as offer a place to use a fire pit for your picnic. In fact, if it's late summer or early fall, and you are a good fisher, this is a popular spot to drop a line in the water to catch your picnic.

Directions

Derby (pronounced Darby) Reach lies along the Fraser River just west of Fort Langley. Access is from the 200th Street exit off Highway 1. Transit doesn't take you right to the park. You must walk, or cycle, along 96th Avenue to McKinnon Crescent, about 2.5 km, to access the trails. Once you are in the park, it's another 4 km to the picnic area.

Notes

Restrooms: These are available at the entrance to the park.

Dogs: Rover must be under control at all times. Both on-leash and off-leash areas exist in the park.

Hollyburn Lodge on Cypress Mountain

Distance: 2 km
Time: 30 min. – 1.5 hrs.
Level: easy
Grade: easy < 75 m
Public Transit Routes: no transit
Surface: snow

Activity Highlight

Hollyburn Lodge is a historic and rustic lodge (though a new lodge design is currently being planned) used as a warming hut, food kiosk and bathroom stop for skiers and snowshoers on Cypress Mountain. On many Saturday evenings, the lodge has live music, which can extend your picnic into an evening meal (cook on your camp stove outside in the snow) with some North Shore culture.

Directions

Begin at the far end of the cross-country ski parking area and take the snowshoe trail. Follow the signs to the lodge. In ten minutes you will be at the first junction – stay left. Another ten minutes and you will be at Hollyburn Lodge. In the winter, a shuttle (for a fee) takes you to the cross-country area. See the start of the snowshoe chapter for more information on getting to Cypress Mountain by shuttle.

Notes

Restrooms: These are available at the lodge.

Dogs: Canine companions are not permitted on the trail to Hollyburn Lodge.

Whytecliff Park in West Vancouver

Distance: 0 km
Time: 0 min.
Level: easy
Grade: easy 0 m
Public Transit Routes: 250, C12
Surface: beach, rock

Activity Highlight

This is a classic spot for sunset picnics as it faces southwest into the Strait of Georgia with views of Bowen Island and Vancouver Island. It's also a great place to watch scuba divers enter and exit the water. If the tide is not too high, you should be able to walk out to the rocky bluff, but pay attention that you aren't cut off by the water before your return.

OPPOSITE: *What ingredients make up the ultimate West Coast picnic? Salmon, perhaps?*
ABOVE: *The picnic divas of the tourism department at Capilano University* (PHOTO COURTESY OF KIM MCLEOD)

Directions

This park is just south of Horseshoe Bay. There is not a walk or a hike component to this park, unless you take transit, and then it's a couple of blocks to walk. Otherwise, the beach is next to the parking area.

Notes

Restrooms: These are available at the base of the stairs where they meet the beach.

Dogs: On-leash dogs are permitted in most areas of this park.

Final Thoughts

This book has provided an overview of many ways to experience Metro Vancouver. Those of us who live in and visit the region are extremely fortunate to have such an area available for our recreational pursuits. The landscape of the region is diverse, while the infrastructure that supports it is excellent. Due primarily to these two factors, its citizens, and visitors, can experience the region in multiple ways. The average British Columbian often takes our roads, transit, ferry system and parkland areas for granted. When they recreate outdoors, their personal safety exploring an area is a virtual guarantee. We may value the educational components our recreational areas provide, and appreciate the commercial operators who help ease our access to it. Then, it seems to me, we often complain about our high taxes and the poor quality of the systems that are in place!

Perhaps, deep down, we believe we can always do better, or maybe we value our systems but would rather others pay for them. However, we choose to look at it, one thing is certain: Metro Vancouver planners have done a great job! Just knowing I can walk out my front door this weekend and choose from a variety of activities, geographic locations, businesses to buy or rent from and clubs or organizations willing to share with me is an amazing testament to what we have accomplished. In addition, knowing I can easily get there via a walking path, on my bicycle, by transit, by driving or by ferry is worth reflecting on. Finally, knowing I feel safe, whether I am on a dedicated cycling path, in a harbour around boats, on a secluded forest trail or swimming in water that won't make me ill is vitally important for a wholesome life. Take time to think about the infrastructure in Metro Vancouver as you embark on your recreational activities. This infrastructure allows me to be a recreational generalist. What does it do for you? Enjoy the outdoors.

"To be whole. To be complete. Wildness reminds us what it means to be human, what we are connected to, rather than what we are separate from."

—Terry Tempest Williams, *Red: Passion and Patience in the Desert*, 2001

Appendix A: Bioregional Quiz

What Do You Know about the Environment That Surrounds You?

In Eco-Insight: Watersheds (page 146), I asked what you know about the infrastructure and natural areas that support and surround you. I once came across a great environmental education handout at the Sea to Sky Outdoor School on Keats Island. Using its idea, I have adapted questions specifically for this book. Here is a short quiz to gauge your knowledge about the infrastructure that surrounds and supports us.

1. Describe a distinguishing feature of the common plants called trillium and maidenhair fern. What purpose might either serve to support or nurture humans?

2. Without looking, do you know what stage the moon is at in the sky tonight? Does it appear to be getting bigger or smaller? What does the moon do that affects our lives substantially? If you are unsure, read the Eco-Insight for Lighthouse Park (page 87).

3. Where does the water come from at your home before it reaches your tap?

4. What direction does most of the weather come from in Metro Vancouver? Why?

5. What has had the greatest influence on the landforms in Metro Vancouver? When did this take place?

6. Where does your wastewater go? How about your garbage or your recycling?

7. What are the most common birds in your neighbourhood? Are these birds migrants or do they stay all year-round?

8. What are three, dominant, native tree species near your home?

9. Can you identify the cloud types overhead right now? What other clouds do you know?

10. What are the names of the First Nations in this region?

TOP: *What phase is the moon in tonight?* (PHOTO COURTESY OF ROB ALEXANDER)

BOTTOM: *How many different types of ferns do you know?*

(PHOTO COURTESY OF RORRI MCBLANE)

What do you know about clams? (PHOTO COURTESY OF VALERIE BELANGER)

Bioregional Quiz Answers

1. A distinguishing feature of a trillium is that it has three leaves and three petals. That is where the "tri" comes from in trillium (look back at the Whyte Lake activity, page 96, for an image of a trillium). The maidenhair fern is quite different from other ferns because it has a black stem and is very feathery or lacy in appearance. As for the purpose of a plant, asking how it supports humans is a question that is easy to get philosophical about. Why does it matter how any plant serves us is my first thought. However, both the maidenhair fern and the trillium serve us in many ways. The fern roots hold soil together near waterfalls, leading to less erosion into water streams. The trillium provides aesthetic beauty in forests and serves as a draw for tourists. Both feed forest species, capture CO_2, detoxify wastes, serve pollinators and provide educational opportunities for countless budding naturalists.

2. Often it is difficult to know what stage the moon is at if it has been overcast for many days. This question is more of a reminder to look at the sky and pay attention to the changes happening overhead. Over a set of clear days, make a point of watching when the moon rises or sets on the horizon. Over that time you will notice its apparent change in size, whether it is waxing (growing and moving toward a full moon) or waning (diminishing and moving toward a new moon) and that it rises and sets a little later each day. A good friend of mine, Rick Davies, provided an easy way to remember the waxing and waning of the moon. Use the letters *D, O* and *C as shapes*: *D* is the waxing, *O* is the full moon and *C* is the waning of the moon. Of course, the moon's biggest effect on our lives is that it is largely responsible for our ocean tides.

3. If you live in Metro Vancouver (with the exception of White Rock), your water comes from one of three watersheds – the Coquitlam, Seymour or Capilano. White Rock gets its water from an underground aquifer. Water from the Capilano and Seymour watersheds goes through the water filtration plant in the Seymour Valley, while water from the Coquitlam watershed is not filtered. The water from all three watersheds is chlorinated at the source, and often rechlorinated along the water pipe lines as it moves to Metro Vancouver homes. All three watersheds are closed to the public to ensure clean and safe drinking water.

4. Most of Metro Vancouver's weather comes from over the Pacific Ocean in the west. This is due to the prevailing winds at this location on the planet.

5. One major influence on the landforms in Metro Vancouver is past glaciation. The glaciers that existed over the area until the glacial retreat about 11,000 years ago sheared off the tops of the local mountains, created the steep sides of the Sea-to-Sky Highway and the fjord of Howe Sound, altered soil conditions, eliminated most vegetation and mammals and created the many north-south valleys and lakes in this region (Pitt, Stave, Harrison lakes and Capilano, Seymour and Coquitlam valleys).

6. Metro Vancouver's wastewater goes primarily to the Iona Island

or the Annacis Island wastewater treatment plants. Garbage and recycling is collected municipally and, depending on the municipality, is disposed of in different ways. Some is shipped to other areas in British Columbia, Washington or globally; some is burned; some is buried; some is reclaimed.

7. The most common year-round birds in most Metro Vancouver neighbourhoods include (but are certainly not limited to) black-capped chickadee, red-breasted nuthatch, Pacific wren, varied thrush, American robin, starling, house sparrow, house finch, song sparrow, downy woodpecker, golden-crowned kinglet, dark-eyed junco, northwestern crow, Steller's jay, pigeon, California gull, mallard, Canada goose and bald eagle. Those that pass through Metro Vancouver on their migrations elsewhere include many warbler, waterfowl, raptor and shorebird species, among others. You can get a bird checklist for Metro Vancouver at the Naturevancouver.ca website. The checklist states what birds are common in this area and during which season.

8. The dominant, native tree species that are familiar in multiple areas around Metro Vancouver include western red cedar, coastal Douglas fir, coastal western hemlock, black cottonwood, red alder, bigleaf maple, paper birch and arbutus.

9. If it is a bright or sunny day, then the cloud types are probably cumulus, cirrus, cirrostratus or altostratus. If it's a rainy day, then the cloud types are probably stratus, nimbostratus or stratocumulus. Finally, if it is a stormy summer day in Metro Vancouver, then the cloud types are probably cumulonimbus.

10. There are several First Nations in Metro Vancouver and their historic territories are generally associated with geographic areas we call municipalities, townships and cities. Though there is overlap, in general, the Nations and their territories include the Katzie (Surrey, Pitt Meadows, Langley); Kwantlen (Langley, Maple Ridge); Kwikwetlem (Coquitlam); Matsqui (Langley); Musqueam (South Vancouver and parts of Delta); Semiahmoo (White Rock); Squamish (North and West Vancouver and the Sea-to-Sky Highway region); Tsawwassen (Delta) and Tsleil-Waututh (North Vancouver

near Deep Cove). For a detailed map, see www.metrovancouver
.org/region/aboriginal/Aboriginal%20Affairs%20documents/
ProfileOfFirstNationsJanuary2014.pdf.

Appendix B: Activities Sorted by Region

If you are looking for an activity in a certain region, use these tables as a guide.

Vancouver-Burnaby Region

Location	Activity Type	Public Transit	Page
Locarno Beach	trail run	4, 84, C19	44
Vancouver Biennale	cycling	SkyTrain/Canada Line	156
Vancouver Seawall to Kits Pool	cycling	SkyTrain/Canada Line	164
Vancouver Shoreline	paddling	SkyTrain/Canada Line	181
Stanley Park	rowing	250 – 254, 257, 258	226
Kits Pool	swimming	2, 22, 32, 258	164
English Bay	stand-up paddleboard	C21, C23	234
Jericho Beach	stand-up paddleboard	C19	234
Burnaby Lake	trail run	110, 134, 144	40
Burnaby Lake	rowing	110, 134, 144	43, 226
Burnaby Mountain Urban Trail	inline skating	145	230
Vancouver-Burnaby Central Valley Greenway	inline skating	SkyTrain/Millennium Line	230

North Shore Region – East to West

Location	Activity Type	Public Transit	Page
Quarry Rock – Deep Cove	hike	211, 212, C15	73

Location	Activity Type	Public Transit	Page
Deep Cove to Jug Island/ Belcarra	canoe/kayak	211, 212, C15	190, 195
Jug Island Beach	picnic	211, 212, C15	195 , 251
Deep Cove	stand-up paddle-board, rowing	211, 212, C15	231
Cates Park	picnic	212	77, 121
Maplewood Flats	walk	212, C15	77, 121
Dog Mountain – Mount Seymour	snowshoe	no transit	112
Dinky Peak – Mount Seymour	snowshoe	no transit	117
Seymour Valley to Old-Growth Forest	cycling	228	143
Seymour Valley Pathway	inline skating	228	227
Seymour Valley River at 9 km	picnic	228	136, 143, 251
Rice Lake	walk	228	116, 143
Lynn Valley – Lynn Loop	trail run	228	61
Lynn Canyon Pools and Suspension Bridge	walk	229	64
North Shore Spirit Trail	inline skating	multiple access points	230
Capilano Canyon	hike	232, 236, 247	78
Grouse Grind	hike	232, 236, 247	82
Bowen Lookout at Cypress Mountain	snowshoeing	no transit	122
Hollyburn Peak at Cypress Mountain	snowshoeing	no transit	127
Hollyburn Lodge	picnic	no transit	130, 263

Location	Activity Type	Public Transit	Page
Cypress Mountain Cross-Country Ski Area	cross-country skiing	no transit	244
Black Mountain at Cypress	hike	no transit	89
West Vancouver Seawall	walk	250, 252, 253	93, 126, 221
Cypress Falls	hike	253, C12	97, 99
Whyte Lake	hike	250	94, 102, 103
Lighthouse Park	hike	250	83
Juniper Point at Lighthouse Park	rock climbing	250	83, 87, 249
Whytecliff Park	picnic	250, C12	88, 265
Crippen Park/Killarney Lake – Bowen Island	trail run	250, 257	65

Tri-Cities-Ridge Meadows Region – East to West

Location	Activity Type	Public Transit	Page
Widgeon Slough and Falls	canoe/kayak	no transit	205
Pitt Polder Dyke	walk	no transit	208
Minnekhada Regional Park	trail run	no transit	57
Traboulay PoCo Trail	cycling, inline skating	159, 160, C37, C38	152
Buntzen Lake	canoe/kayak	190, C26 "Buntzen Lake Special" in summer only	185

Location	Activity Type	Public Transit	Page
Sasamat Lake – Belcarra Park	swimming	150 in summer only, C26 Port Moody/ Belcarra	212
Admiralty Point – Belcarra Park	picnic	150 in summer only, C25, C26 Port Moody/ Belcarra	256
Jug Island Beach – Belcarra Park	hike	150	198

Delta-Richmond Region – North to South

Location	Activity Type	Public Transit	Page
Richmond Loop	cycling	SkyTrain/Canada Line	160
Garry Point Park and Steveston	cycling	401, 402, 407, 410	161, 163
George C. Reifel Migratory Bird Sanctuary	walk	no transit	56
Boundary Bay Dyke	cycling	601, 603, 604, C84	138
Brunswick Point	trail run	620	52
Point Roberts	cycling	SkyTrain/Canada Line, 601, 602	147
Lily Point – Point Roberts	picnic	SkyTrain/Canada Line, 601, 602	147, 251

Surrey-White Rock Region – East to West

Location	Activity Type	Public Transit	Page
Barnston Island – Surrey	picnic	no transit	239
White Rock Beach	stand-up paddleboard	354, C52	234
Crescent Beach – Surrey	swimming	351	216
Nicomekl River	canoe/kayak, rowing	351, 375	200, 226

Location	Activity Type	Public Transit	Page
Boundary Bay Dyke	cycling	351, 352, 354	138
Centennial Beach Park	walk	351	151

Fraser Valley Region

Location	Activity Type	Public Transit	Page
Campbell Valley	trail run	531, C63	48
Fraser Valley Local Food and Wine	cycling	531, C60 – C63	169
Strawberry Flats at Manning Park	cross-country ski	no transit	244

Go Further: Squamish-Whistler Region

Location	Activity Type	Public Transit	Page
Stawamus Chief	hike	no transit	104
Paul Ridge in Garibaldi Park	snowshoe	no transit	131
Rock Climbing and Bouldering in Squamish	rock climbing	no transit	245
Callaghan Valley	cross-country skiing	no transit	240
Lost Lake – Whistler	cross-country skiing	no transit	244
Squamish Estuary	walk	no transit	108

Go Further: Sunshine Coast, Strait of Georgia & Vancouver Island Region

Location	Activity Type	Public Transit	Page
Salt Spring Island to Ganges	walk	BC Ferries (Tsawwassen to Galiano, Mayne, Pender, Salt Spring and Saturna islands)	217
Lochside Trail – Vancouver Island	cycling	BC Ferries (Tsawwassen-Swartz Bay)	174

(PHOTO COURTESY OF JENN DICKIE)

Location	Activity Type	Public Transit	Page
Mount Gardner on Bowen Island	hike	250, 257 BC Ferries (Snug Cove-Horseshoe Bay)	69
Galloping Goose from Victoria – Sooke	cycling	BC Ferries (Tsawwassen-Swartz Bay), 72, 76, 81	178
Sidney to San Juan Island	cycling	BC Ferries (Tsawwassen-Swartz Bay), 72, 76, 81	178

Appendix C: Dog-Friendly Activities

These activities are in locations that either have special accommodations for dogs or are areas your dog will thank you for bringing them to! Use this table as a guide.

Activity	Notes	Page
Skiing in the Callaghan Valley	There are dog-specific trails to ski with your pooch.	240
Buntzen Lake Paddle	If you take a canoe to Buntzen, and your dog likes water, then this may be a good place to introduce your pet to canoeing. However, when the dog is out of the boat at North Beach, it must be on-leash. South Beach has an off-leash area.	185
Lighthouse Park Hike	Dogs are allowed off-leash but must remain under control.	83
Cypress Falls Hike	Dogs are allowed off-leash but must remain under control.	99
Traboulay PoCo Trail Cycle Loop	There are dog parks around parts of this loop that allow off-leash dogs.	152
Whytecliff Park Picnic	Dogs must be on-leash on the beach but can play in the ocean.	265
Barnston Island Picnic or Walk	The loop road is mostly quiet and easy to walk or cycle with your pet, but be sure it is under your control as there are farm animals on Barnston Island.	259
Quarry Rock Hike	Dogs are allowed off-leash but must remain under control.	73
Burnaby Lake Run	There is an off-leash area at Warner Loat near the north entrance of the park. This is an easy park to run your dog on-leash if you do the 10-km loop.	40

Activity	Notes	Page
Crippen Park – Bowen Island Run	A mix of off- and on-leash areas on Bowen Island can easily be found.	65
Locarno Beach Run	When the tide is out, there is a vast expanse of beach for your pet to run along.	44
Dog Mountain Snowshoe	This snowshoe is on-leash, but it is fairly easy to have your dog accompany you while on snowshoes. Moreover, with a name like Dog Mountain, how could you leave your pet at home?	112

Appendix D: Group Activities

The following activities are grouped based on the company that would be suited to join you on the activity. These include activities with children, teenagers, older adults and visitors.

Activities with Children

These children-appropriate activities are suggested due to the level of physical activity required, other child-oriented interests associated with them, or for the sense of accomplishment the child will have upon completion.

Activity	Notes	Page
Quarry Rock Hike	This offers a challenge with interesting bridge crossings and a great view. Upon returning, children will feel a sense of triumph as they look up to the high point while you treat them to a post-hike doughnut in Deep Cove!	73
Burnaby Lake	This is for young children who have an interest in feeding ducks and visiting a nature house. There is a good possibility they will see beavers in the water at sunset too.	42
Bowen Lookout Snowshoe	This provides a challenge over a fairly short snowshoe to an amazing view on a clear day. A lodge at the end of your activity serving hot chocolate helps end this snowshoe on a different sort of high point.	122
Dinky Peak Snowshoe	Another easy, short snowshoe that you can scope out for a future family, snow-cave, overnight excursion.	117
Seymour Valley Pathway Cycle	This is for active children who like to cycle and are comfortable cycling hills and over some distance. They will feel a sense of accomplishment with this ride.	143
Widgeon Slough Paddle	Children will love the opportunity to get out of the boat and walk alongside it if it's the summer and the tide is low. They will also enjoy seeing salmon in the water in the fall.	205

Use this book when looking for activities to do with children and teens. This is me and my sons Christopher and Brent atop Stawamus Chief in Squamish.

Activities with Teenagers

These teen-appropriate activities are suggested due to the level of physical activity required, their "cool" factor and the sense of accomplishment the teen will have upon completion.

Activity	Notes	Page
Black Mountain Summit Hike	This is a challenging climb that often parallels a downhill ski run on Cypress. Teenagers will feel pride at the top then have a riot running down the ski hill in the summer. There's a great view from the top too!	89
Stawamus Chief Hike	If there is any one hike that will turn a teen on to hiking, this is it! Get them to the rocky bluff and let them stand in awe at the vertical cliff below their feet!	104

Activity	Notes	Page
Rowing Sculls	Delta Deas and many other rowing clubs offer youth programs and allow teens to try out the sport.	222
Widgeon Slough Paddle	The child in every teen will want to get out of the boat and walk alongside it, while the teen in them will see the falls as a great place to bring friends back to.	205
North Shore Mountain Biking	Find a teen who wants to show you what they know on a bike, or who you can introduce these new trails to.	235

Activities with Older Adults

These older-adult-appropriate activities are suggested due to the degree of physical activity required, including how level the landscape is and the ease of the activity on the bones and muscles. In addition, they are all beautiful areas.

Activity	Notes	Page
Crippen Regional Park on Bowen Island – as a Hike	This is an easy, undulating walk through deciduous forest with many turn-around points. As a bonus, there are multiple places to stop in Snug Cove for food and drinks.	65
Rowing Sculls	This is a great older-adult sport as it is easy on the joints.	222
Cypress Mountain, Bowen Lookout Snowshoe	This short but somewhat challenging snowshoe provides a great view and a sense of success at the high point (but it's not too high!). A lodge upon your return is useful too.	122
Boundary Bay Cycle	This flat and easy ride (if it isn't windy) provides views, birds and a way to ride side by side while talking.	138
Barnston Island Picnic	A 1.5-km walk to a picnic table overlooking the Fraser River provides a great spot to share old stories and watch the working river.	259

Activity	Notes	Page
Callaghan Valley Ski	Cross-country skiing is a great sport that is easy on the joints while providing fresh air and exercise.	240

Activities with Visitors

These visitor-appropriate activities are suggested due to their beauty and tourism relevance.

Activity	Notes	Page
Vancouver Seawall Cycle	You can't have new visitors to Vancouver and not bring them to the gem of the city – the Vancouver Seawall.	164
Vancouver Shoreline	It would be difficult to find a paddle more urban than False Creek to English Bay in Vancouver's West End. However, if you are looking for a West Coast, urban, kayak experience, this may be it.	181
Lochside Trail Cycle	For active visitors who want to also visit Victoria, this is an alternate way to get there and avoid ferry line-ups and traffic congestion. Remember, you can put two bikes on a transit bus to return.	174
Salt Spring Island Walk	Gulf Islands National Park Reserve is one of Canada's newest parks. The park is not part of this walk, but the ecosystem is. Show your visitors why by walking with them in this unique Canadian ecosystem.	217
Deep Cove – Jug Island Paddle	If the water in Indian Arm is calm, your visitors are fit and you have some experience kayaking, this activity pairs the community of Deep Cove with some spectacular West Coast beauty.	195
Dinky Peak Snowshoe	This site is easy to get to and requires little effort, but it has amazing views.	117
Admiralty Point Picnic	Belcarra Regional Park is a gem in the regional park system. This point in the park is the crown of that gem. On the right day, it is truly a highlight picnic area in Metro Vancouver.	256

Appendix E: Activities Sorted by Difficulty Level

If you are looking for an activity in a certain difficulty level, then use this table as a guide.

Difficulty Level	Region	Distance/Time	Page
Trail Running			
easy	Burnaby Lake – Burnaby	11 km/1 – 1.5 hrs.	40
easy	Locarno Beach – Vancouver	5 – 10 km/45 min. – 2 hrs.	44
easy	Campbell Valley – White Rock	5 – 10 km/1 – 2 hrs.	48
easy	Crippen Park – Bowen Island	9 km / 1-1.5 hrs.	65
moderate	Brunswick Point – Delta	8 – 15 km/1 – 2.5 hrs.	52
moderate	Lynn Loop – North Vancouver	5 km/1 – 1.5 hrs.	61
moderate	Minnekhada – Coquitlam	5 – 10 km/35 min. – 2 hrs.	57
Hiking			
easy	Cypress Falls – West Vancouver	3 km/1 – 1.5 hrs.	99
easy – moderate	Lighthouse Park – West Vancouver	4 – 6 km/1.5 – 2.5 hrs.	83
moderate	Quarry Rock – North Vancouver	3.5 km/1.5 – 2 hrs.	73
moderate	Capilano Canyon Loop – North Vancouver	6 km/2 – 3 hrs.	78
moderate	Whyte Lake – West Vancouver	6 km/1.5 – 2 hrs.	94
difficult	Black Mountain – West Vancouver	6 km/4 hrs.	89
difficult	Stawamus Chief – Squamish	4 km/2.5 – 3.5 hrs.	104

Difficulty Level	Region	Distance/Time	Page
Snowshoeing			
easy	Dinky Peak – North Vancouver	2.1 km/30 min. – 1.5 hrs.	117
moderate	Dog Mountain – North Vancouver	6 km/1.5 – 2 hrs.	112
moderate	Bowen Lookout – West Vancouver	3 km/1 – 2 hrs.	122
difficult	Hollyburn Peak – West Vancouver	7 km/ 3 – 4 hrs.	127
difficult	Elfin Lakes Trail to Paul Ridge – Squamish	14 km/ 4 – 6 hrs.	131
Cycling			
easy	PoCo Trail – Port Coquitlam	25 km / 1.5-2 hrs.	152
easy	Fraser Valley Local Food and Wine – Langley	25 km / 1.5-2 hrs.	169
moderate	Boundary Bay Dyke – Delta/Surrey	40 km / 2.5-3 hrs.	138
moderate	Seymour Valley Pathway – North Vancouver	23 km / 2-3 hrs.	143
moderate	Point Roberts, WA, Cycle Loop – Delta/Point Roberts	20 km/1 – 2.5 hrs.	147
moderate	Vancouver Biennale – Vancouver	15 – 60 km/1 – 4 hrs.	156
moderate	Richmond Loop – Richmond	33 km/2 – 3 hrs.	160
moderate	Seawall to Kits Pool – Vancouver	42 km/2.5 – 3.5 hrs.	164
moderate	Lochside Trail – Vancouver Island	66 km/full day	174
Paddling			
easy	Buntzen Lake – Coquitlam	6 – 7 km/1.5 – 2.5 hrs.	185
easy	Nicomekl River – South Surrey	7.5 – 9.5 km/3 – 5 hrs.	200
easy	Vancouver Shoreline	5 – 13 km/2 – 5 hrs.	181

Difficulty Level	Region	Distance/Time	Page
moderate	Deep Cove – Belcarra – North Vancouver/Coquitlam	6 km/2 – 3 hrs.	190
moderate	Deep Cove – Jug Island – North Vancouver	5.5 km/2 – 3 hrs.	195
	Other Adventures		
easy – moderate	Sasamat Swim – Coquitlam	1 – 2 km/30 min. – 1 hr.	212
easy – moderate	Cross-Country/Skate Skiing – Whistler	5 – 20 km/1 – 4 hrs.	240
moderate	Walking Salt Spring Island – Gulf Islands	12 – 15 km/full day	217
moderate	Rock Climbing and Bouldering in Squamish	full day	245
moderate	Stand-Up Paddleboarding – North Vancouver	1 – 3 km/1 – 2 hrs.	231
moderate – difficult	Rowing – Deas Island Park, Ladner	3 – 12 km/2 hrs.	222
difficult	Inline Skating – North Vancouver	19 km/1.5 – 3 hrs.	227
	Active Picnic Adventures		
easy	Admiralty Point at Belcarra – Coquitlam	3 km/1 hr.	256
easy	Barnston Island – Surrey	3.5 – 10 km/20 min. – 1 hr.	259
easy	Kanaka Creek – Maple Ridge	1 – 3 km/15 – 45 min.	260
easy	Hollyburn Lodge – West Vancouver	3 km/30 min. – 1.5 hrs.	263
moderate	Seymour River at 10 km – North Vancouver	18 km/2.5 hrs.	145

Bibliography

Baron, N., and J. Acorn. *Birds of Coastal British Columbia: And the Pacific Northwest Coast*. Edmonton: Lone Pine, 1997.

Butler, R.W. *The Jade Coast: Ecology of the North Pacific Ocean*. Toronto: Key Porter Books, 2003.

Cannings, R.J., and S.G. Cannings. *The BC Roadside Naturalist*. Vancouver: Greystone Books, 2002.

———. *British Columbia: A Natural History*. Vancouver: Greystone Books, 1996.

Clague, J.J., and B. Turner. *Vancouver, City on the Edge: Living with a Dynamic Geological Landscape*. Vancouver: Tricouni Press, 2003.

Eifert, L. *Field Guide to Old-Growth Forests: Exploring Ancient Forest Ecosystems from California to the Pacific Northwest*. Seattle: Sasquatch Books, 2000.

Grescoe, A. *Giants: The Colossal Trees of Pacific North America*. Vancouver: Raincoast Books, 1997.

Kricher, J.C., and G. Morrison. *A Field Guide to the Ecology of Western Forests*. Boston: Houghton Mifflin, 1993.

MacKinnon, A., J. Pojar, and P.B. Alaback. *Plants of Coastal British Columbia including Washington, Oregon & Alaska*. Edmonton: Lone Pine Pub, 2004.

Mathews, D., and the Audubon Society of Portland. *Cascade-Olympic Natural History*. Portland, OR: Raven Editions in conjunction with the Audubon Society of Portland, 1988.

McDonald, R. "Old Growth, New Death." [Radio series episode]. *Quirks and Quarks*. Canadian Broadcasting Corporation.

Metro Vancouver. *Profile of First Nations*. January 1, 2014. http://www.metrovancouver.org/region/aboriginal/Aboriginal Affairs documents/ProfileOfFirstNationsJanuary2014.pdf.

Murray, A., and D.P. Blevins. *A Nature Guide to Boundary Bay*. Delta, BC: Nature Guides BC, 2006.

Suzuki, D.T., R. Bateman, W. Grady, and the David Suzuki Foundation. *Tree: A Life Story*. Vancouver: Greystone Books, 2004.

Tap Water. January 1, 2014. http://www.metrovancouver.org/region/Pages/TapWater.aspx.

The Mighty Fraser. January 1, 2009. http://www.fraserriverdiscovery.org/aboutthefraser.

The Salmon Forest. USA: Bullfrog Films, 2001.

Index

About the Author

Roy Jantzen is a professor of natural history at Capilano University in the Faculty of Tourism and Outdoor Recreation. He has a lifelong passion for local ecosystems and the species that inhabit them. In addition, Roy also has a strong desire for exercise and recreation and sees Metro Vancouver as one of the most accessible regions on the planet for nearby green spaces to facilitate this. Holding a master of arts in environmental education and communication through Royal Roads University, Roy believes that all education can be environmental education. His passions have helped fill his life with an equal amount of conservation and environmental education work. Beginning with leading tours to Clayoquot Sound and the Carmanah Valley, near Victoria, BC, decades ago, to helping educate the public about the importance of these biodiverse areas, to immersing his post-secondary students in ecotourism or alpine ecosystems, Roy has always sought to connect our use of the natural world to the importance of its preservation.

Currently, Roy is temporarily living in Yukon. There, he is helping to expand the public's knowledge of northern Canada's Peel River watershed as a board member of the Yukon Conservation Society. He has also worked with Yukon College and Tourism Yukon to design wilderness tourism workshops for new entrepreneurs, and he has worked with the Climate Change Secretariat on the Yukon's Climate Change Action Plan. However, as so many northerners do, he balances his Yukon work with exploring the territory's many natural wonders through hiking, biking, canoeing and skiing.